ORU Class of 2022

With my prayer for the special presence of the Holy Spirit's empowering work upon you

Following Jesus:
Spirituality of Disciples

Copyright © 2019 by Dr. Young Hoon Lee

All rights reserved. No part of this book may be reproduced in any form without the written permission of the publisher, with the exception of brief excerpts in printed reviews.

All Scripture quotations in this publication are from the HOLY BIBLE, NEW INTERNATIONAL VERSION ® NIV ® Copyright © 1973, 1978, 1984, 2011 by Biblica, Inc.®. Used by permission. All rights reserved worldwide.

The "NIV" and "New International Version" are trademarks registered in the United States Patent and Trademark Office by Biblica, Inc.®.

Use of either trademark requires the permission of Biblica, Inc.®.

Following Jesus: **Spirituality of Disciples**

LOGOS USA, INC

3268 Smithtown Road, Suwanee, GA 30024

Printed in Korea

ISBN 978-1-7341273-0-0 52000

Following Jesus:
Spirituality of Disciples

Young Hoon Lee

logos

Preface

The era of spirituality has come. People try to overcome the limit of man's intellect and sensibility through their spirituality in this era of swift change and insecurities. However, the pursuit for spirituality with wrong directions has led people to mysticism, new age movement, heresies, or pseudo-religions, misleading them. Materialism, extreme individualism, and the conflicts between generations reveal the present state of their ruined spirituality.

In this stream of times, we must pursue the spirituality of Jesus—the spirituality to follow Jesus, which is based on the teachings of the Bible. As Christians, we should try to imitate and follow Jesus throughout our lives. We must love, obey, and humbly serve others and the whole community as Jesus did.

Then we will enjoy true satisfaction and joy that the world cannot offer.

This book is the compilation of my short sermons on various broadcasting programs, reconstructed under the eight themes of this book, *Following Jesus: the Spirituality of Disciples*.

I pray that this book will lead its readers to be filled with the spirituality of the disciples of Jesus, spreading out dreams and hope all around.

What is the spirituality of disciples?

The spirituality of disciples seeks similarity to Jesus. It is the spirituality with which we obey as Jesus obeyed God, humbly serving our neighbors and society. There are eight characteristics in the spirituality of disciples.

1. The spirituality of the cross
- The cross is the completion of the love of God and the foundation of the eternal salvation for all humankind.
- We must follow the way of the cross of Jesus until we meet Him.

2. The spirituality of the Word
- Christian spirituality is thoroughly founded on the

Word of God.
- The Word is the ultimate standard in our faith and life.

3. The spirituality of the fullness of the Holy Spirit

- We can understand the love and grace of God through the work of the Holy Spirit. Also, we can receive Jesus as the Savior through the Spirit.
- We need the help of the Spirit to become mature Christians.

4. The spirituality of prayer

- Prayer is the spiritual channel through which the joy of heaven is brought into our hearts.
- God answers our prayers and leads our lives through our prayers.

5. The spirituality of absolute, positive faith

- Salvation we received leads us to have absolute, positive faith.
- Absolute, positive faith is based on the Word of God, the suffering on the cross and the resurrection of Jesus,

eternal heaven that is allowed to us through Jesus, and the hope for the second coming of Jesus.

6. The spirituality of service and sharing

- Living a life of service and sharing is committing our way to the Lord by putting down everything we have rather than living as the master of our own lives.
- Since we have received unconditional grace and blessings from God, we must share what we have with others without sparing anything.

7. The spirituality of personal sanctification

- We must follow the Lord Jesus to become true Christians as written: "Follow my example, as I follow the example of Christ" (1 Corinthians 11:1).
- We must love one another, forming harmony, dedicating ourselves for salvation, and seeking godly and holy life.

8. The spirituality of missionary work

- Jesus commanded His disciples, "Go into all the world and preach the gospel to all creation" (Mark 16:15) before

He ascended to heaven.

- We must preach the gospel with all our might in season or out of season.

Contents

Preface
What is the spirituality of disciples?

Part 1 The spirituality of the cross • 13

1 Crowd or Disciple
2 The Love of the Cross
3 The Cross of Jesus

Part 2 The spirituality of the Word • 41

4 The Seed That Fell on Four Kinds of Soil
5 The Word and Faith
6 The Voice of God

Part 3 The spirituality of the fullness of the Holy Spirit • 67

7 A Voice of One Calling in the Wilderness
8 Were Not Our Hearts Burning
9 Only by the Holy Spirit

Part 4 The spirituality of prayer • 97

10 A Great Mother
11 Have Mercy on Me
12 The Grace at the Ford of the Jabbok

Part 5 The spirituality of absolute, positive faith · 123

- 13 Be Strong and Courageous
- 14 Faith That Makes Impossible Things Possible
- 15 Quiet! Be Still!

Part 6 The spirituality of service and sharing · 151

- 16 The Greatest of These Is Love
- 17 What Should We Do
- 18 Those Whom God Loves

Part 7 The spirituality of personal sanctification · 179

- 19 With Christ
- 20 God Who Is Always with Us
- 21 The Chosen One

Part 8 The spirituality of missionary work · 207

- 22 The Hope of Resurrection
- 23 Mission
- 24 March forward with Dreams and Hope

1

Following Jesus: Spirituality of Disciples

The spirituality of the cross

1. Crowd or Disciple

2. The Love of the Cross

3. The Cross of Jesus

01

Crowd or Disciple

> *Then he called the crowd to him along with his disciples and said: "Whoever wants to be my disciple must deny themselves and take up their cross and follow me."* (Mark 8:34)

Many people live aimlessly, not knowing where they came from, what they're living for, or where they're headed. For this reason, they feel empty. But we, who've become God's children by claiming that Jesus is Lord, obtained the clear goal of life. We found the reason for our existence, the purpose in life. What is this purpose? Jesus gave His disciples the Great Commission before He was taken up to heaven.

Therefore go and make disciples of all nations, baptizing

them in the name of the Father and of the Son and of the Holy Spirit. (Matthew 28:19)

The purpose of our existence on this earth is to follow the Great Commission—to make disciples of all nations. How? First, we must become Jesus' disciples ourselves. Today's Bible Scripture throws three questions at us so that we could check whether we are true disciples.

1. Are we the crowd or the disciples?

Mark 8:34 begins with Jesus "call[ing] the crowd to him along with his disciples." Note that there are two groups: the crowd and the disciples. Here, the crowd consisted of people who have experienced or witnessed the miracles that Jesus performed and followed Him for the miracles. In other words, they followed Jesus for their own benefit or satisfaction.

The story where Jesus feeds five thousand men with just five loaves of bread and two small fish is written in all of the four Gospels; including women and children, the crowd consisted of at least 20,000 people. Jesus said to them, "very truly I tell you, you are looking for me, not because you saw the signs I performed but because you ate the loaves and had your fill" (John 6:26).

Jesus knew that the crowd followed Him because they were fed and satisfied and not because they realized Jesus was the Messiah. The crowd wasn't interested in who He truly was, but in the miracles that He performed.

Kyle Idleman of Southeast Christian Church said the following in his book, *Not a Fan*, that fans are those who "cheer for [Jesus] when things are going well ... [and] walk away when it's a difficult season." [1]

Who Jesus wants aren't those who cheer for Him by looking at His miracles. Jesus wants those who follow His words and dedicate themselves wholly to Him. The crowd who followed Jesus was only entranced with His miracles. Initially, when Jesus entered Jerusalem, they took palm branches and spread them out, shouting, "Hosanna to the Son of David" (Matthew 21:9), but when they realized that Jesus was not a political leader they wanted Him to be, they turned their backs from Him.

Are you a crowd or a disciple? In Matthew 6:33, Jesus tells

us to "seek first his kingdom and his righteousness, and all these things will be given to [us] as well." We shouldn't follow the Lord Jesus for our satisfaction; we should seek the kingdom and the righteousness of God. We must wholly dedicate ourselves to Him.

2. Whose disciple do we want to be?

Jesus said to the crowd: "Whoever wants to be my disciple must … follow me" (Mark 8:34). Who should we follow? Jesus and no one else. People claim that they follow Jesus yet they still chase after worldly pleasures such as money and power. If you truly follow Jesus, you can't have other idols in your life.

The things on earth are evanescent and disappointing. When we follow worldly things, we'll end up empty-handed. When we follow people, they are bound to hurt us and leave us in despair.

For instance, think about the Samaritan woman of Sychar. She'd been married five times but none of her marriages were successful. She was currently living with a man without getting married. It's evident that her life was filled with dissatisfaction and misery. Abashed, she wanted to escape the eyes of her villagers.

We can't find satisfaction in other people. True satisfaction only comes from Jesus our Lord. True satisfaction only comes to us when we follow Jesus.

Jesus' disciples gave up all things and followed Him. When Jesus called Peter, Andrew, James, and John, who were fishermen, they instantly put down their nets and followed Jesus. Matthew, a tax collector, gave up his job for Jesus. They may have seemed foolish from the worldly point of view, but they chose a joyful life and they were greatly used for the glory of God.

Following Jesus is accompanied by sacrifice and pain, but it also leads you to true joy. When you follow people or the patterns of this world, you'll ultimately end up disheartened. Don't look to this world or people but look to the Lord Jesus alone and follow Him.

3. What kind of life should we live?

Mark 8:34b says that we "must deny [ourselves], take up [our] cross and follow [Jesus]."

There are two elements in the discipleship: to deny oneself and to take up his or her cross. Calvin the Reformer said that these two are the core elements in Christian life.

To deny ourself means to confess that we are nothing and Jesus is everything, then continually practicing this confession.

People feed off of their own pride. They think the world is their oyster; the world revolves around them. Therefore, they thrive with praise or validation but get offended when others chastise them. If we're dead in the Lord and Christ lives in us, nothing can hurt or offend us. We can always live victoriously through Jesus.

To take up our cross means to endure any suffering or sacrifice that may occur to us as we follow Jesus. As Jesus says that "whoever does not take up their cross and follow [Him]" are unworthy of His love, we can't follow Him without suffering or sacrificing for Him (Matthew 10:38).

Thomas à Kempis described the cross that Christians should take in his book, *The Imitation of Christ*, as follows:

> The cross, then, is always ready and waits for you in every

place. You cannot escape it wherever you run. For wherever you go you carry yourself with you, and you will always find yourself. Look up or look down; look out or look in; and in all directions you will find the cross. And so, it is necessary for you to be patient everywhere, if you wish to have interior peace and merit the eternal crown. If you bear the cross willingly, it will bear you and lead you to the desired end, to that place where suffering will end, a place impossible to find here on earth.[2]

Where there is no cross, there is no crown. No sacrifice, no blessing. God won't bless us with grace and mercy if we refuse to suffer for Christ. Please remember that Jesus was resurrected in His glory since He bore His cross.

Jesus' disciples didn't escape the cross either. According to the tradition of the early church, Peter, asserting that he was unworthy to be crucified in the same manner as his Lord, was nailed to the cross upside down. Apostle Paul was beheaded. Bartholomew was skinned alive. Thomas was martyred in India and stabbed by a spear. But they didn't fear death because they followed the way of the cross willingly and thankfully.

Those who don't know Jesus are unhappy. They don't have a set direction in life. But we have a patent purpose: to live for God's glory and for the gospel.

We have clear goals on this earth. We must become true disciples of Jesus first, then make disciples throughout our lives. It's our purpose as Christ's ambassadors. It's the reason of our existence. Fix your eyes on the Lord. Follow Jesus. Deny yourself and take up your cross. Then the season of Jesus Christ will be established on this earth through you.

02

The Love of the Cross

> *Jesus replied: "'Love the Lord your God with all your heart and with all your soul and with all your mind.' This is the first and greatest commandment. And the second is like it: 'Love your neighbor as yourself.' All the Law and the Prophets hang on these two commandments."* (Matthew 22:37-40)

The cross is the core of Christian faith—the promise of redemption for all humankind was completed on the cross. Jesus Christ, the only Son of God, came to this earth, became sin, and died on the cross. Through His death on the cross, we were given the grace of salvation, the Holy Spirit, and bountiful blessings from God.

The cross is composed of two lines: one vertical and one horizontal. The former signifies the love for God while the latter refers to the love for our neighbors. Therefore, as the children of God, we must love God and our neighbors.

An expert in the law tested Jesus with this question: "Which is the greatest commandment in the Law?" (Matthew 22:36). Jesus replied to him, citing the two commandments: love God and love one's neighbors. This is the love that the cross teaches us.

1. Love for God

Jesus says: "Love the Lord your God with all your heart and with all your soul and with all your mind. This is the first and greatest commandment" (Matthew 22:37-38).

We must love our God with all our hearts and with all our souls and with all our minds. Why do we have to love God this way? Because God loves us and adopts us as His children even though we're sinful, filthy, and troubled.

Apostle Paul says that "God demonstrates his own love for us in this: While we were still sinners, Christ died for us" (Romans 5:8).

God's love for us was verified by the cross. Wouldn't we be very grateful if someone pays off our debt? Jesus paid our debt on the cross. He paid the price of sin, which we can't possibly pay with our own capability. Shouldn't we give much more thanks to Him?

Only those who are thankful can love God with all their hearts and with all their souls and with all their minds. They can live for God's glory, giving thanks to Him for His grace of salvation.

What is the purpose of our existence? Isaiah 43:7 says this: "Everyone who is called by my name, whom I created for my glory, whom I formed and made." Indeed, we were created for the glory of God. Only God should receive glory through what we do.

Apostle Paul also exhorted the church of Corinth in his letter, saying, "So whether you eat or drink or whatever you do, do it all for the glory of God" (1 Corinthians 10:31). When we shift our focus to giving glory to God, He will bless us abundantly.

2. Love for our neighbors

Matthew 22:39 says: "And the second is like it: 'Love your

neighbor as yourself.' "

Jesus' standard regarding brotherly love is this: we should love our neighbor as we love ourselves. We love ourselves and take great care of ourselves. We spend a lot of money and time on improving our looks and health. For instance, some Koreans are eager to eat almost anything if it is good for their health. Just like how we take care of ourselves, we should lavishly do so for our neighbors.

Loving our neighbors isn't easy. It's especially hard to love those who hurt us or bring us down. However, Luke 6:32-33 says: "If you love those who love you, what credit is that to you? Even sinners love those who love them. And if you do good to those who are good to you, what credit is that to you? Even sinners do that."

We rebelled against God and turned away from Him, living in sin. In spite of our rebellion, God loved us and still loves us. Though we were doomed to die due to our sins, God loved us so much that He sent Jesus to die on the cross so that we may be saved. Even though we broke His heart, He never turned His face away and held us in His arms filled with vast love.

When we become God's beloved children, we experience

mercy. God forgave our dreadful sins. Hence, we should be eager to love and forgive those who have caused pain in our lives.

During the Last Supper, Jesus said to His disciples: "A new command I give you: Love one another. As I have loved you, so you must love one another. By this everyone will know that you are my disciples, if you love one another" (John 13:34-35). When we love one another, it's evident that we're Jesus' disciples.

3. The practice of love

True love means sacrifice. If not accompanied by sacrifice and its practice, it's not love. Jesus sacrificed His own life on the cross to save us. He fed the hungry. He healed the sick. By putting His love into practice, He set an example of love.

1 John 3:17-18 says: "If anyone has material possessions and sees a brother or sister in need but has no pity on them, how can the love of God be in that person? Dear children, let us not love with words or speech but with actions and in truth." If we truly love God, we should share what we have with those

who are less fortunate than we are. The more we share love, the more plentiful our love will become. The more we give with generosity, the more we'll experience God's love. This is because God pours His grace on us more when we share our blessings with others.

Paul remarks in Romans 13:9-10:

The commandments, "You shall not commit adultery," "You shall not murder," "You shall not steal," "You shall not covet," and whatever other command there may be, are summed up in this one command: "Love your neighbor as yourself." Love does no harm to a neighbor. Therefore love is the fulfillment of the law.

Indeed, love is the fulfillment of the Law, and we can accomplish God's will by putting love into practice. What is the greatest implementation of love? You display your love by preaching the gospel. It will be the greatest execution of your love if you lead nonbelievers to Christ. If your parents are non-Christians, what do you think is the best way to show your love for them? You should help them look to Christ and experience His love. You're fulfilling His love by doing your best to preach the gospel of the Lord to whom you love.

We'll eventually leave this world and stand before the Lord. Then, what will you say to Him? You should be able to say, "I loved God and my neighbors while I was on earth." As Jesus said that all the Law and the Prophets hung on these two commandments—loving God and loving our neighbor (Matthew 22:40), we need to actively try to love God and share that love with our neighbors. Then God will receive glory from us, and many will come to the Lord when we leave beautiful marks of love.

03

The Cross of Jesus

> *But he was pierced for our transgressions, he was crushed for our iniquities; the punishment that brought us peace was on him, and by his wounds we are healed.*
> (Isaiah 53:5)

Jesus was nailed on the cross for the redemption of mankind from sin. Through His sacrifice and love on the cross, we are now God's children. He blesses His children both spiritually and physically—even our surroundings are blessed! Therefore, to live as faithful Christians, we must understand the meaning of the cross and experience its grace every day.

Around 700 B.C., Prophet Isaiah prophesied about the suffering of Jesus in great detail. He spoke about four ways of His suffering in Isaiah 53:5. Let's follow Jesus' footsteps in

His suffering and give thanks to Him for His grace that was manifested on the cross.

1. Jesus has forgiven our transgressions.

The first part of Isaiah 53:5 tells us that "[Jesus] was pierced for our transgressions." Here, by "our transgressions," Isaiah means the sinfulness of mankind, for man turned away from God and rebelled against Him. It's graver than simple mistakes due to man's weakness; it's man's arrogance towards God.

Isaiah 1:2 says: "Hear me, you heavens! Listen, earth! For the Lord has spoken: 'I reared children and brought them up, but they have rebelled against me.'" As Isaiah points out, we're so arrogant that we have rebelled against God, living debauchedly and unrighteously.

Jesus wore the crown of thorns on His head so that He could bring forgiveness on our numerous transgressions. When sharp thorns pierced His head, He shed His blood with indescribable pain. One of the soldiers pierced Jesus' side with a spear, bringing a sudden flow of blood and water. He suffered until the last drop of His blood was shed. God sent Jesus to this earth so that we may be forgiven from all our transgressions, and Jesus loved us enough to shed all of His blood and to die on the cross.

It wasn't the Roman soldiers who set the crown of thorns on His head, it was us. Because of our transgressions, His side was pierced with a spear. Therefore, we must give constant thanks to Jesus for His grace, who suffered in our place to forgive our transgressions.

2. Jesus took our iniquities.

The second part of Isaiah 53:5 also tells us that "[Jesus] was crushed for our iniquities." Here, being crushed means that all the bones were out of joint and completely shattered.

Psalm 22:14, where the Psalmist writes from the Lord's perspective regarding His suffering, says: "I am poured out like water, and all my bones are out of joint. My heart has turned to wax; it has melted within me." Jesus must have felt the utmost pain in every joint. He was crushed. His appearance was disfigured so badly that "there were many who were appalled at him—his appearance was so disfigured beyond that of any human being and his form marred beyond human likeness" (Isaiah 52:14).

Why in the world did Jesus have to suffer even though He was sinless? He suffered because of our sins and iniquities. Because we didn't live in accordance with God's will. Because we followed our desires and lived self-centeredly. Isaiah 53:6 says that "We all, like sheep, have gone astray, each of us has turned to our own way; and the Lord has laid on him the iniquity of us all."

God, with the heart of a father, never gives up on us His children. Psalm 103:13 says: "As a father has compassion on his children, so the Lord has compassion on those who fear him." God forgives our sins and iniquities with the compassion and love of a father. To solve the problem of our sins, God gave His one and only Son Jesus to us. Through Jesus' death on the cross, all our sins are forgiven. This signifies the Lord's love manifested on the cross. Therefore, give thanks to the Lord for His love manifested on the cross and live obediently to God's will.

3. Jesus brought peace to us.

The third part of Isaiah 53:5 contends that "the punishment that brought us peace was on him." Since Jesus was punished in our place, we are reconciled to God and we have peace.

Isaiah 59:2 says: "But your iniquities have separated you from your God; your sins have hidden his face from you, so that he will not hear." Adam and Eve were expelled from the Garden of Eden and were separated from God because they sinned against Him. The relationship between God and man was totally broken.

Man can't mend the broken relationship between God and him by himself. However, Jesus became the High Priest and recovered our relationship with God that had been broken. So even though we are weak and vile, we can approach God. Hebrews 10:19-22 says: "Therefore, brothers and sisters, since we have confidence to enter the Most Holy Place by the blood of Jesus, by a new and living way opened for us through the curtain, that is, his body, … let us draw near to God."

The moment Jesus said "it is finished" on the cross, the veil that separated us from God was torn. Now, we can approach

God with confidence. Since Jesus was punished for and instead of us, we're reconciled to God. We're given true peace in our lives.

So to enjoy peace with God, we must come to the cross every day. True peace is given to us only through the cross. Always experience and enjoy true peace by Jesus' love shown on the cross.

4. Jesus heals us.

The last part of Isaiah 53:5 reminds us that "by his wounds, we are healed." Jesus shed His blood to heal us. He was whipped, which left stripes on His body, for us.

Jesus had compassion on those who were afflicted. He had mercy on them and healed them. According to the Gospels, He devoted two thirds of His public ministry to healing the sick. Jesus went throughout Galilee, teaching in synagogues, proclaiming the good news of the kingdom, and healing every disease and sickness among the people.

Jesus was afflicted because He loved us and wanted to

rescue us from sickness. 1 Peter 2:24 says that "He himself bore our sins in his body on the cross, so that we might die to sins and live for righteousness; by his wounds you have been healed."

The whips that the Romans soldiers used had lead beads and sharp animal teeth attached at the tip. When one was hit with a whip, his or her flesh was torn off. Jesus was hit by these whips and His flesh was torn off, causing His blood to gush out.

Why should Jesus suffer so much even though He was sinless? He wanted to heal all sickness and weakness that had been caused by the sin of mankind. By the wounds and stripes on His body, our spirits and our souls and our bodies are healed. The curses on our surroundings are lifted.

Jesus is with us now and He wants to heal us. Hebrews 13:8 says that "Jesus Christ is the same yesterday and today and forever." Therefore, we must go to the cross, for Jesus is the great healer and everlasting doctor. Go to Jesus with your sickness and be healed by the Lord Jesus. Gain a new life from Him.

Jesus was pierced by thorns and spears for our transgressions.

He was crushed for our iniquities. He was punished to bring peace to us. He was whipped to heal us. Therefore, even if we go through these kinds of sufferings, we shouldn't lose heart. We must go to the cross with confidence, fighting our diseases by His name and by the power of His blood. We must fight and overcome sin. Enjoy the victory that Jesus accomplished on the cross.

St. Francis and the Leper

Saint Francis feared and hated lepers, which was natural since no one wanted to catch a contagious disease. But one day, shortly after his conversion, he met a leper near Assisi. Francis was in conflict: though the sight of the leper filled him with disgust, he had a desire to go and pray for him.

With fear, he turned away from the leper. It was then the Holy Spirit made him feel the burden. Francis stopped and prayed.

"I passed by the man with an affliction. Was it wrong?" he asked.

The Lord answered, "why did you pass by him?"

"I was afraid because he was so filthy and I might catch the disease."

"Are you any better than the filthy leper? You were even filthier sinner than the man. I accepted you the way you were and loved you."

That moment, Francis realized once again that God saved him with love even though he was a wretched sinner more filthy than was the leper. So he went to the leper, embraced him, kissed him and prayed for him. This was just the beginning. He went down to the colony of lepers and became their friend. He cared for and kissed their wounds, living as their friend.

His last words were: "Jesus, my love and everything."

2

Following Jesus: Spirituality of Disciples

The spirituality of the Word

4. The Seed That Fell on Four Kinds of Soil

5. The Word and Faith

6. The Voice of God

04

The Seed That Fell on Four Kinds of Soil

That same day Jesus went out of the house and sat by the lake. Such large crowds gathered around him that he got into a boat and sat in it, while all the people stood on the shore. Then he told them many things in parables, saying: "A farmer went out to sow his seed. As he was scattering the seed, some fell along the path, and the birds came and ate it up. Some fell on rocky places, where it did not have much soil. It sprang up quickly, because the soil was shallow. But when the sun came up, the plants were scorched, and they withered because they had no root. Other seed fell among thorns, which grew up and choked the plants. Still other seed fell on good soil, where it produced a crop—a hundred, sixty or thirty times what was sown. Whoever has ears, let them hear." (Matthew 13:1-9)

We all have the same Christian faith but some bear more fruit than others do. Those who don't bear fruit can't display the power of God in their lives. There's no growth. On the other hand, those who bear much fruit in the Lord receive and enjoy more of God's abundant grace and blessings. God blesses those who bear much fruit for His glory and leads their lives.

We can find the theory behind this in Jesus' parable of the sower. A farmer went out to sow his seed. As he was scattering the seed, some fell along the path, some fell on rocky places, some fell among thorns, some fell on good soil. Only the seed that fell on good soil produced a crop—a hundred, sixty or thirty times what was sown. In this parable, the sower refers to God, seed the word of the gospel, and four kinds of soil the minds of the listeners. Through this parable of the sower, let's examine the state of our hearts and think about how we can apply this in our lives so that we may be rooted in the good soil.

1. The seed that fell along the path

Matthew 13:4 says that "some [seed] fell along the path, and the birds came and ate it up." In Jesus' days, the farmers in the Philistine area wore seed bags around their waist and scattered the seed from October to November, the rainy season. When wind blew while the sower was scattering the seed, some of the seed fell along the path. Since many people walked on the path, the seed couldn't take root in it. So the birds came and ate it up.

Matthew 13:19 says: "When anyone hears the message about the kingdom and does not understand it, the evil one comes and snatches away what was sown in their heart. This is the seed sown along the path." This case of the parable signifies that the Word can't take root in a person who has heard the gospel yet still has a hardened heart. Satan will come and snatch it away.

When the grace of God comes upon us as we listen to the Word, it takes root in our hearts, grows, and produces crops. But those who've gone through a lot in this world often have trouble accepting God's grace because their hearts have hardened throughout. Those who commit sin habitually also have hardened hearts and the Word can't take root in their hearts. If we have a heavy heart, we must plow the soil thoroughly with the bulldozer of repentance.

Hosea 10:12 says: "Sow righteousness for yourselves, reap the fruit of unfailing love, and break up your unplowed ground; for it is time to seek the Lord, until he comes and showers his righteousness on you." We must come to the Lord and thoroughly repent, turning away from our sinful lives. We must recognize our spiritual powerlessness and an indifference to His grace. Then God will plow our hardened hearts, producing a good crop. I pray that God will pour the spirit of repentance on you so that your hearts will be renewed.

2. The seed that fell on rocky places

Matthew 13:5-6 says that some seed "fell on rocky places, where it did not have much soil. It sprang up quickly, because the soil was shallow. But when the sun came up, the plants were scorched, and they withered because they had no root."

Since soil in Israel is composed mainly of limestone, there are many rocky places. When a seed falls on rocky places, it could spring up quickly on the shallow soil. But since the soil is so shallow, the plants will be scorched when the sun comes up.

Ultimately, they will wither because they have no roots.

Jesus says: "The seed falling on rocky ground refers to someone who hears the word and at once receives it with joy. But since they have no root, they last only a short time. When trouble or persecution comes because of the word, they quickly fall away" (Matthew 13:20-21). Those who have hearts like rocky places hear the Word and receive it with joy. However, it only lasts for a while. When trouble comes, they get frustrated and quickly fall away. Since they have the rocks of hatred, resentment, or regrets, the Christian faith can't take root in them.

Therefore, we must get rid of the rocks from our hearts. Jeremiah 23:29 says: "'Is not my word like fire,' declares the Lord, 'and like a hammer that breaks a rock in pieces?'" We must break the rocks into pieces with the hammer of the Word. Unless we remove these rocks from our hearts, the rocks will become heavy burdens throughout our lives, pressing us down heavily.

We all have some rocks in our hearts whether we recognize it or not—the rocks of hatred, hurts and wounds, or anger. Break those rocks into pieces with the Word so that your hearts will turn into good soil.

3. The seed that fell among thorns

Matthew 13:7 says that "other seed fell among thorns, which grew up and choked the plants." Due to Israel's arid land, many thorny bushes grow near their farmland. Since thorns are so prolific, they grow very quickly and choke other plants. The seed that fell among thorns couldn't grow well or produce good crops.

This seed refers to one who hears the Word but whose faith doesn't grow spiritually because of thorns like anxiety or greed. Jesus says: "The seed falling among the thorns refers to someone who hears the word, but the worries of this life and the deceitfulness of wealth choke the word, making it unfruitful" (Matthew 13:22). These thorns keep the Word from working in their lives.

Only the fire of the Holy Spirit can burn and consume the thorns. The fire will drive away these sinful thoughts from our hearts. We must receive the fullness of the Holy Spirit so that our faith will grow every day.

4. The seed that fell on good soil

Matthew 13:8 says: "Still other seed fell on good soil, where it produced a crop—a hundred, sixty or thirty times what was sown."

This seed refers to someone who hears the Word and understands it. This is the one who produces fortuitous crop, yielding much more than what was sown. When our hearts turn into good soil, God profusely pours out His wonderful grace and blessings on us.

We've examined the four kinds of soil. We may have rocks of wound, heavy hearts, or thorns. We must get these problems solved before God. When we repent of our sins and meditate on the Word, our hardened hearts will be plowed. The rocks in our hearts will be broken into pieces. When we are filled with the Holy Spirit through our fervent prayers, the fire of the Spirit will burn all the thorns in our hearts. Then our hearts will turn into good soil. God will bless us greatly and exhibit His glory all over the world through us. Make every effort to produce a crop more than what's sown by becoming the good soil.

05

The Word and Faith

Consequently, faith comes from hearing the message, and the message is heard through the word about Christ. (Romans 10:17)

Christian faith is initiated and completed by Jesus, so we must put Jesus first—from the beginning through the end. Our hearts should become like Jesus, we should manifest the Lord Jesus in our lives, and the work of Jesus should be accomplished in everything we do. To become His servants who emulate Jesus, we should be filled with faith and the faith should take deep root in the Word of God.

1. We must listen to the voice of the Lord every day.

Romans 10:17 begins with: "Consequently, faith comes from hearing the message."

We hear many things, but most voices we hear from this world or from people are depressing. But the voice of the Lord always gives us joy, peace, healing, and forgiveness. Our souls are revived when we hear the voice of the Lord.

John 10:27-28 says: "My sheep listen to my voice; I know them, and they follow me. I give them eternal life, and they shall never perish; no one will snatch them out of my hand." Since we're the Lord's flock, we need to listen to His voice. Since the Lord is with us and takes good care of us, no one can snatch us out of His hand.

We hear the voice of the Lord when we worship Him. John 4:23-24 says: "Yet a time is coming and has now come when the true worshipers will worship the Father in the Spirit and in truth, for they are the kind of worshipers the Father seeks. God is spirit, and his worshipers must worship in the Spirit and in truth." God looks for true worshipers and speaks to them.

We should also be aligned with Scripture and meditate on

it because we hear the voice of the Lord through the Word. Psalm 119:103 says: "How sweet are your words to my taste, sweeter than honey to my mouth!" and Psalm 1:1-2 says: "Blessed is the one who does not walk in step with the wicked or stand in the way that sinners take or sit in the company of mockers, but whose delight is in the law of the Lord, and who meditates on his law day and night."

We must do our best in worshipping Jesus and admiring the Word. We experience the grace and healing from God when we worship our Lord with all our hearts and with all our souls and with all our minds. The Word will free us by breaking all the shackles. We need to worship the Lord with all our hearts and admire the Word of God.

2. We must stand firmly on the Word.

We must stand firmly on the Word and listen to His voice. Romans 10:17b says: "The message is heard through the word about Christ."

Jesus Christ alone is the hope for human beings. There isn't another way to salvation except through Him. For this reason, in John 14:6, Jesus answers: "I am the way and the truth and the life. No one comes to the Father except through me." He also says in John 5:24: "Very truly I tell you, whoever hears my word and believes him who sent me has eternal life and will not be judged but has crossed over from death to life."

The entire Bible testifies to the power of Jesus' blood. The blood is sprinkled on the entire Bible from Genesis 1:1 through Revelation 22:21 and thus sprinkled on our hearts as we read the Bible. Our wounds will heal. All our problems will be resolved. Miracles will happen. This is the power of the blood of Jesus.

His blood also becomes the foundation of the forgiveness of our sins. When Adam and Eve sinned, God made garments of skin for them. They saw the sinless animal being slaughtered for their sins. This symbolizes Christ's death on the cross. Even though Jesus was sinless, He died on the cross and opened the door of salvation for us.

Hebrews 9:22 says: "In fact, the law requires that nearly everything be cleansed with blood, and without the shedding of blood there is no forgiveness." Since Jesus died on the cross, shedding His blood, whoever believes in Him can be saved and be filled with the Holy Spirit. Experience the power of the blood of Jesus and be filled with the Holy Spirit by listening to the Word, trusting it and counting on it.

3. We must march forward with faith.

After being armed with His Word and the power of His blood, we must march forward with faith. Romans 10:17 says: "Consequently, faith comes from hearing the message, and the message is heard through the word about Christ." God will bless us when we march forward with faith.

We can have faith when we hear Jesus' voice. The voice we hear from the Lord is the Word of God and Jesus is the main character of the entire Bible. Our life will turn into the blessed life when we meet the Lord Jesus. When we hear His voice we're transformed in Him.

As Christians, we live our entire life with the faith in Jesus. We're saved by believing in Jesus. We fight sin by being filled with the Holy Spirit. As the precious and faithful servants of the Lord, we should put the love of Jesus into practice in our daily life.

About the wonderful work of faith, Matthew 17:20 says: "He replied, 'Because you have so little faith. Truly I tell you, if you have faith as small as a mustard seed, you can say to this mountain, "Move from here to there," and it will move. Nothing will be impossible for you.'"

The world history is carried on by those who have dreams, those who believe that their dreams will come true. Hebrews 11:1 says that "faith is confidence in what we hope for and assurance about what we do not see." Miracles and blessings will come to us when we believe and march forward with faith.

Even if something looks impossible to our eyes, if we hold onto our absolute, positive faith and march forward, impossibility becomes possibility. Problems turn into the blessings of God.

Hebrews 11:6 states that "without faith it is impossible to please God, because anyone who comes to him must believe that he exists and that he rewards those who earnestly seek him," and Romans 8:28 says that "we know that in all things God works for the good of those who love him, who have been called according to his purpose." Therefore, we must march forward with faith, holding onto the Word of God. Even if we encounter tribulations in our lives, be armed with faith and listen to nothing but His voice. Hold onto the Word and trust the power of the cross.

Faith comes from hearing the message. So try to hear the message of the Lord during worship services. Listen to the Word, read it, and meditate on it every day. Experience the power of the cross through the Word. Great and marvelous things will happen in your life and you will become God's precious servants, giving glory to Him.

06

The Voice of God

When the woman saw that the fruit of the tree was good for food and pleasing to the eye, and also desirable for gaining wisdom, she took some and ate it. She also gave some to her husband, who was with her, and he ate it. Then the eyes of both of them were opened, and they realized they were naked; so they sewed fig leaves together and made coverings for themselves. Then the man and his wife heard the sound of the Lord God as he was walking in the garden in the cool of the day, and they hid from the Lord God among the trees of the garden. But the Lord God called to the man, "Where are you?" He answered, "I heard you in the garden, and I was afraid because I was naked; so I hid." (Genesis 3:6-10)

We hear many voices. The devil tries to steal, kill, and destroy us with its whispers of sweet temptations. This world is under the power and authority of the devil, and people are the slaves to sin. These people hurt us, but the voice of God always gives us dreams and hope. It revives us, heals us, and comforts us with His love and forgiveness. We shouldn't listen to the voice of the world or the people in this world, but open our spiritual ears to hear His voice. When we listen to the Word and obey it, we can live victoriously.

The first humans—Adam and Eve—were living a blessed life in the Garden of Eden, having fellowship with God. However, they listened to the serpent, fell into temptation, and sinned. Let us think about the spiritual lessons through this episode.

1. The voice that Eve heard

After God created the whole world and everything in it, He created Adam, took him and put him in the Garden of Eden so that he could take care of the garden. There was only one thing that God forbade him. Genesis 2:16-17 says: "And the Lord God commanded the man, 'You are free to eat from any tree in the garden; but you must not eat from the tree of the knowledge of good and evil, for when you eat from it you will certainly die.'"

God created Adam and gave him free will so that he could judge and decide for himself. God wanted him to live a life that was pleasing to God with his free will. That's why God put the tree of the knowledge of good and evil in the garden though He forbade him from eating it. The tree signifies the sovereignty of God. Eating from the tree meant a grave sin and crime that violated the sovereignty of God.

Then the Lord God caused Adam to fall into deep sleep, and while he was sleeping, He took one of his ribs and made a woman, Eve, from the rib He had taken out of him.

One day, the serpent, under the control of Satan, came to Eve and raised questions regarding the fruit of the tree. Genesis 3:4-5 says: "'You will not certainly die,' the serpent said to the woman. 'For God knows that when you eat from it your eyes will be opened, and you will be like God, knowing good and evil.'" Satan was deceiving. It tempted her and told her that she would be like God.

Eve became prideful when she heard Satan's voice. Genesis 3:6 says that "when the woman saw that the fruit of the tree was good for food and pleasing to the eye, and also desirable for gaining wisdom, she took some and ate it. She also gave some to her husband, who was with her, and he ate it."

Deceived by the devil, and hoping that they could become like God, Eve ate the fruit and gave some to Adam. They broke God's command.

Man's desire to become like God is pride, the root of all sins. Solomon, the wisest man on earth, tells us that "pride goes before destruction, a haughty spirit before a fall" (Proverbs 16:18). God detests the proud. He accomplishes His marvelous work through the humble. Don't listen to the devil lest pride should come into your minds. We must always serve our God with humility.

2. The voice that Adam heard

Genesis 3:8 says: "Then the man and his wife heard the sound of the Lord God as he was walking in the garden in the cool of the day, and they hid from the Lord God among the trees of the garden."

After Adam and Eve sinned, they heard God's voice. Ashamed, they hid from Him among the trees of the garden. They were afraid because sin had entered into their hearts. But God asked them: "where are you?" (Genesis 3:9). God didn't ask this question because He didn't know where the man was. He didn't call him because He wanted to judge or condemn him. God called him because He wanted to give him and his wife a chance to repent by asking, "What are you doing now? What kind of relationship do you have with me right now?"

We must always listen to the voice of God. When the Lord asks, "Where are you? What are you doing? What kind of relationship do you have with me right now?" we should be able to answer Him, "Lord, here I am. I love you. I am always trying to serve you and live for your glory."

When God called him, Adam should have repented of his sins by saying, "Lord God, I sinned. Forgive me," but he didn't. Instead, he threw the entire blame on his wife. Genesis 3:12 tells us that Adam said, "The woman you put here with me—she gave me some fruit from the tree, and I ate it." Eve, in turn, blamed the serpent.

We shouldn't blame others when we have sinned. Psalm

34:18 says that God is "close to the brokenhearted and saves those who are crushed in spirit." When we hear God calling us, we must kneel down before Him and repent. God forgives us when we repent. Don't shut your ears when you hear His voice. Stop making excuses. Come to the cross, confess your sin, and repent. Live for the glory of God.

3. The voice of God we hear from the cross

Since Adam and Eve didn't show remorse, God punished them. Man would eat from the ground through painful toil, and woman's pains in childbearing became very severe. Her husband was going to rule over her.

This wasn't the only consequence of sin. Since their spirits were dead, their relationship with God was severed. They'll be afflicted by sickness and then return to the ground, which was cursed because of them. This three-fold punishment came upon man as the consequence of his sin.

Nevertheless, God, with His infinite love, showed man the way to be forgiven. Genesis 3:21 says: "The Lord God made garments of skin for Adam and his wife and clothed them." God had mercy on them even though they sinned against Him, and He killed a sinless animal for them. He made garments of skin for them and clothed them. He established the sacrifice of blood. Following this tradition, the Israelites offered animal sacrifices—the sacrifice of blood—to bring atonement.

This sacrifice of blood symbolically signifies the sacrifice of Jesus Christ—His shed blood and His death on the cross for our sins. Through His death on the cross, Jesus offered the sacrifice of redemption once and for all. Now, whoever believes in Him will be forgiven. Hebrews 9:22 says: "in fact, the law requires that nearly everything be cleansed with blood, and without the shedding of blood there is no forgiveness."

Therefore, when we approach God and trust in the blood of Jesus, God will bless us spiritually, physically, and environmentally. We'll enjoy the three-fold blessing of God, being freed from the three-fold punishment. Listen to His voice through the cross. We have to make resolutions to serve God alone. Then we'll have the overflowing grace of salvation.

God's voice not only brings dreams and hope in our hearts,

but it also helps us look to the future. It helps us create new history. So don't listen to the negative voice from the world nor follow it. Don't be shaken by listening to the voice of people in the world. Listen to the voice of God from the cross and live a life of humility and obedience. March forward with absolute, positive faith and thanksgiving. Listen to His voice, rejoice in Him, and praise Him always.

Another Dimension of Healing, Biblical Oriental Medicine

Elder Yang-Kyu Kim was born into a Christian family. He had tuberculosis in college and went through a cardiac operation after graduation. He began to doubt God and His existence after his near-death experience, but he read through the Bible more than 60 times and met God. Further, he found the connecting link between the Bible and the oriental medicine. He said the following in his book, *The Biblical Oriental Medicine*:

The oriental medicine cures the body of the patient but as Christians, we must act like medical doctors and control our minds and souls with the Word every day. When we control our souls and stand firmly on the Word, our hearts will be automatically under control. Christians cultivate their minds with love, gratitude and joy by controlling their minds with the Word. Our souls will be cured and all anxiety, worry, insecurity, fear and negative thoughts will be cast out.

3

Following Jesus: Spirituality of Disciples

The spirituality of the fullness of the Holy Spirit

7. A Voice of One Calling in the Wilderness

8. Were Not Our Hearts Burning

9. Only by the Holy Spirit

07

A Voice of One Calling in the Wilderness

As it is written in Isaiah the prophet: "I will send my messenger ahead of you, who will prepare your way"— "a voice of one calling in the wilderness, 'Prepare the way for the Lord, make straight paths for him.'" And so John the Baptist appeared in the wilderness, preaching a baptism of repentance for the forgiveness of sins. The whole Judean countryside and all the people of Jerusalem went out to him. Confessing their sins, they were baptized by him in the Jordan River. John wore clothing made of camel's hair, with a leather belt around his waist, and he ate locusts and wild honey. And this was his message: "After me comes the one more powerful than I, the straps of whose sandals I am not worthy to stoop down and untie. I baptize you with water, but he will baptize you with the Holy Spirit." (Mark 1:2-8)

Everyone's born to live, but Jesus was born to die for our sins instead of us. From the beginning, Jesus' life was a one-way path towards His death on the cross. Before Jesus started His public ministry, John the Baptist prepared the way for Jesus, baptizing people in the wilderness. Let's look at how the grace of God was present throughout the story of John the Baptist.

1. We must prepare the way for the Lord.

Mark 1:2-3 says: "As it is written in Isaiah the prophet: 'I will send my messenger ahead of you, who will prepare your way'—'a voice of one calling in the wilderness, "Prepare the way for the Lord, make straight paths for him."'"

Malachi 3:1 also says: "'I will send my messenger, who will prepare the way before me. Then suddenly the Lord you are seeking will come to his temple; the messenger of the covenant, whom you desire, will come,' says the Lord Almighty."

Most prophets in the Old Testament called people to prepare for the Lord—the Messiah. The Israelites desperately longed for the Messiah, who they thought would give them peace, joy, and freedom and who would deliver them out of deep despair. We, too, must prepare the way for the Lord, eagerly waiting for Him.

The Old Testament prophets called out: "Prepare the way for the Lord, ⋯ a highway for God" (Isaiah 40:3). When a king went off to war, they dispatched an advance party to prepare the road for the king. They would lower the hills, fill the valleys, remove rocks and stones, and make rough roads smooth. In the same way, we must prepare the way for the Lord Jesus—the King of kings and the Lord of lords—in our hearts. We need to prepare our hearts for Him by lowering the hills of our pride and greed, filling the valleys of hatred, and making our rough personality smooth and gentle.

Nothing is a greater blessing than Jesus' coming into our hearts. People can't get out of their problems because they act like the master of their lives, trying to solve their problems on their own. If they continue to do so, their problems will accumulate and consequently confine them. We need to lift up our eyes and behold Jesus who is our eternal hope. Only in Jesus is there hope. Only in Jesus is there life. Don't be disheartened because of worldly matters. Never fight or hate one another. Open your heart and behold the Lord, and march forward with faith.

2. We must repent.

Mark 1:4-5 says: "And so John the Baptist appeared in the wilderness, preaching a baptism of repentance for the forgiveness of sins. The whole Judean countryside and all the people of Jerusalem went out to him. Confessing their sins, they were baptized by him in the Jordan River."

John the Baptist urged others to "repent, for the kingdom of heaven has come near" (Matthew 3:1). Jesus also emphasized the importance of repentance at the beginning of His public ministry, telling them to repent.

Therefore, the gospel we must preach is the message of repentance. We need to urge people to repent and receive Jesus Christ as their Savior. Since everybody is in sin, we can't experience God's grace unless we come to Him with broken hearts. Unless we turn from sin and run to Christ, we can't meet Him.

When John the Baptist preached the importance of

repentance, many people came to him, confessed their sins and were baptized. Mark 1:5 says that "the whole Judean countryside and all the people of Jerusalem went out to him. Confessing their sins, they were baptized by him in the Jordan River."

μετάνοια (metanoia) is "repentance" in Greek. It means to turn around or to change directions. Repentance means the complete change in life as if a man, going Eastbound, turns around and goes Westbound. When we are born again, we must let go of the patterns of our old life and turn around completely. If you keep sinning while saying, "I shouldn't do this," you haven't fully repented. You're feeling guilty, and guilt can't change you. God will delight in us only when we turn to Him. When we repent, God forgives us and rejoices over us. For example, when the prodigal son returned home after squandering all his money, his father held a feast for him. The father says: "Quick! Bring the best robe and put it on him. Put a ring on his finger and sandals on his feet. Bring the fattened calf and kill it. Let's have a feast and celebrate. For this son of mine was dead and is alive again; he was lost and is found" (Luke 15:22-24).

To prepare the way for our Lord Jesus, we must repent of our sins thoroughly. When we repent, we are brought back to life. So will our homes, church and country. I pray that all the churches and Christians in Korea repent so that they can be newly transformed in the Lord.

3. We need to be filled with the Holy Spirit.

Mark 1:8 says: "I baptize you with water, but he will baptize you with the Holy Spirit." After we repent, we must be filled with the Holy Spirit in order to live victoriously. Before He was taken up to heaven, Jesus commanded His disciples to be baptized with the Holy Spirit. It says in Acts 1:4-5:

> On one occasion, while he was eating with them, he gave them this command: "Do not leave Jerusalem, but wait for the gift my Father promised, which you have heard me speak about. For John baptized with water, but in a few days you will be baptized with the Holy Spirit."

Acts 2:1-4 says:

When the day of Pentecost came, they were all together in

one place. Suddenly a sound like the blowing of a violent wind came from heaven and filled the whole house where they were sitting. They saw what seemed to be tongues of fire that separated and came to rest on each of them. All of them were filled with the Holy Spirit and began to speak in other tongues as the Spirit enabled them.

Around 120 followers of Christ obeyed this command and devoted themselves to prayer after the Ascension. The Holy Spirit entered their hearts and they began to speak in other tongues. When the Holy Spirit comes upon us, we'll receive power. When we receive power, we'll become the witnesses of the gospel. Acts 1:8 says: "but you will receive power when the Holy Spirit comes on you; and you will be my witnesses in Jerusalem, and in all Judea and Samaria, and to the ends of the earth."

Receiving the Holy Spirit once isn't enough. We must receive the Spirit again and again. Ephesians 5:18 tells us not "to get drunk on wine, which leads to debauchery…[but to] be filled with the Spirit."

The continuous work of the fullness of the Holy Spirit can

be found in the history of the Pentecostal movement. The Pentecostal movement began with the Azusa Street Revival in Los Angeles, California about 110 years ago. The Holy Spirit fell on William Seymour, a son of freed slaves, and there were numerous testimonies of divine healing and speaking in tongues. A local newspaper reported that a spiritual earthquake happened in Los Angeles.

When we're filled with the Holy Spirit, we can become powerful Christians. Our inner being will become like Jesus and our outer being will become the witness of the gospel. We're living in the era of the Holy Spirit. We can't fulfill the task that God has given to us if we haven't received the Holy Spirit. I pray that the fire of the Holy Spirit will blaze up so that a great revival will take place in the Korean churches and the churches all around the world.

Nothing is a greater blessing than for us to have Jesus as the Master of our life and to obey Him in our daily life. Look deeply into your heart and repent. Receive the Holy Spirit and live as God's faithful servants to preach the gospel. Only then can we stand before the Lord without shame.

08

Were Not Our Hearts Burning

When he was at the table with them, he took bread, gave thanks, broke it and began to give it to them. Then their eyes were opened and they recognized him, and he disappeared from their sight. They asked each other, "Were not our hearts burning within us while he talked with us on the road and opened the Scriptures to us?" They got up and returned at once to Jerusalem. There they found the Eleven and those with them, assembled together and saying, "It is true! The Lord has risen and has appeared to Simon." Then the two told what had happened on the way, and how Jesus was recognized by them when he broke the bread. (Luke 24:30-35)

Many people followed Jesus when He was alive, but when He died on the cross, they were so disappointed that they scattered. So did the two disciples who appeared in this episode of Luke 24.

Let's study the spiritual lessons that Jesus gives to us through the example of the two disciples, who had left Jerusalem, going to a village called Emmaus.

1. What it means by going down to Emmaus

Luke 24:13 says: "Now that same day two of them were going to a village called Emmaus, about seven miles from Jerusalem." Two disciples left Jerusalem and were going down to Emmaus. To leave Jerusalem and to go down to Emmaus in a spiritual sense means that they left Jesus. It's the same as a man walking down on the path to hopelessness. When we remain in Jesus, we'll overcome all kinds of problems. When we leave God's presence, we'll fall into despair that continually worsens.

We find a similar case in the parable of the prodigal son in Luke 15. His father was a rich man and the son had everything he could ask for. But one day, the son asked his father for his share of the estate, and the father divided his property between his two sons. Not long after that, the prodigal son got together all he had and set off for a distant country. He must've thought that he would still enjoy wealth and freedom far away from home, but he recklessly spent his money in wild living. After he had spent everything, he was hired to feed pigs. He was so hungry that he tried eating the pods that the pigs ate. This prodigal son shows the mankind who goes far away from God. When man turns away from God, he will lose everything in the end. He's bound to lament in deep anguish.

Leaving Jesus also means that we're going downhill in our Christian faith. In Luke 10, there was a man who was attacked by robbers while he was going down from Jerusalem to Jericho, which is equivalent to leaving God's loving arms to go into the world. When we leave Jesus, we're bound to fall into robbers' hands. The devil, in the previous case the robber, takes away our health, joy and wealth, leaving us in a miserable state.

Where are you heading? Are you walking on the spiritual downhill path due to your problems in your personal life, in your homes, or in your businesses? Don't worry. Even if you feel like you're facing an impasse, a dead-end, heaven is open for you. Lift up your eyes and behold God. Come back to Him. Cry out to Him. Then He will listen to your prayers and work greatly.

2. Jesus always walks with us.

Jesus went to these two disciples, but they couldn't recognize Him for their eyes were blocked.

Luke 24:15-16 says that "as they talked and discussed these things with each other, Jesus himself came up and walked along with them; but they were kept from recognizing him." Jesus was right there beside them, but they couldn't recognize Him because they were seized by sorrow though they'd followed Jesus for a long time, listened to Him, experienced His grace, and witnessed the miracles He had performed.

Even today, many people fail to recognize Jesus, who is right there beside them. They sigh and complain, saying things like "I'd rather die" and "I have no hope."

Even when you feel suicidal, never forget that Jesus is

right there beside you. He never leaves you. From the day you came to believe in Him until you go to heaven, the Lord Jesus is always with you to guide you through. Open your spiritual eyes, your eyes of faith, and recognize Jesus who is right there beside you.

In 2 Kings 6, the king of Aram sent horses and chariots and a strong force to Dothan to capture Elisha the prophet. An army with horses and chariots surrounded the city. When Elisha's servant got up and went out early the next morning, an army with horses and chariots had surrounded the city. "Oh no, my lord! What shall we do?" the servant asked (2 Kings 6:15). Elisha answered, "Don't be afraid," and prayed to God, saying, "open his eyes, Lord, so that he may see" (2 Kings 6:16-17). The Lord opened the servant's eyes, and he saw the hills full of horses and chariots of fire all around Elisha.

The two disciples who went down to Emmaus recognized Jesus when their spiritual eyes were opened. Luke 24:30-31 says: "When he was at the table with them, he took bread, gave thanks, broke it and began to give it to them. Then their eyes were opened and they recognized him, and he disappeared from their sight."

In the same way, when your spiritual eyes are opened, you'll see that Jesus was right there all along. You're not alone nor are you forsaken or thrown into loneliness. Jesus will never leave you.

3. Jesus sends us the Holy Spirit.

It says in Luke 24:32: "They asked each other, 'Were not our hearts burning within us while he talked with us on the road and opened the Scriptures to us?'" When Jesus talked with them, their hearts were burning by the work of the Holy Spirit.

Like this, the Holy Spirit makes our hearts burn, gives us the assurance of salvation, fills us with faith and courage so that we can live victoriously. This is the reason Jesus appeared to His disciples after He'd resurrected and told them to receive the Holy Spirit. John 20:22 says: "and with that he breathed on them and said, 'Receive the Holy Spirit.'"

What the disciples needed the most was to receive the Holy Spirit. We need to receive the Holy Spirit, too. Only when we receive the Holy Spirit, our hearts can be burning. Only when our hearts are burning, we can pray, truly worship the Lord, and go out and preach the gospel to other people.

After Jesus had resurrected, the disciples were all together in the Upper Room, devoting themselves to prayer. Then the fire of the Holy Spirit fell on them. Before they received the Holy Spirit, they were hiding behind shut doors, but they now went out and preached the gospel. They boldly spoke the Word of God as the Spirit enabled them, and thousands of people were added to their number on a single day.

Those who receive the fire of the Holy Spirit have burning hearts. Their spirits and lives change.

Receive the Holy Spirit like the two disciples who were going down to Emmaus. The Holy Spirit lets your hearts burn and makes you into God's great servants.

God uses those who are filled with the Holy Spirit. When we're filled with the Spirit, God will pour out His grace and blessings that we've never experienced before. Enjoy enormous blessings of God by being filled with the Holy Spirit.

09

Only by the Holy Spirit

While Apollos was at Corinth, Paul took the road through the interior and arrived at Ephesus. There he found some disciples and asked them, "Did you receive the Holy Spirit when you believed?" They answered, "No, we have not even heard that there is a Holy Spirit." So Paul asked, "Then what baptism did you receive?" "John's baptism," they replied. Paul said, "John's baptism was a baptism of repentance. He told the people to believe in the one coming after him, that is, in Jesus." On hearing this, they were baptized in the name of the Lord Jesus. When Paul placed his hands on them, the Holy Spirit came on them, and they spoke in tongues and prophesied. There were about twelve men in all. (Acts 19:1-7)

Now that we've become God's children, we need to be filled with the Holy Spirit so that we can live victoriously. Jesus' disciples were still fearful even after they'd met the resurrected Jesus. Before Jesus was taken up to heaven, He told His disciples not to leave Jerusalem but to wait for the gift that God had promised. They held onto this word and devoted themselves to prayer.

Ten days later, on the day of Pentecost, they experienced the strong outpouring of the Holy Spirit. It totally changed them. They became bold and confident, quite different than they were before they'd received the Holy Spirit. When they preached the gospel after receiving the power of the Spirit, numerous people repented and returned to Jesus. The early Christian Church was born on the day of Pentecost and the era of the Holy Spirit began.

What we need the most today is also the fullness of the Holy Spirit. We must be filled with the Spirit in order to live a powerful Christian life and preach the gospel all around the world as the witnesses of Christ. Let's examine what we will become like when we are filled with the Holy Spirit.

1. We must become the people of the Holy Spirit.

Ephesus was the center in Apostle Paul's third missionary journey. It was the harbor city in Asia Minor, the center of economy, transportation, and trade. The city enjoyed opulence and prosperity but the people worshipped idols centered on the shrines of Artemis.

Paul went to Ephesus and met some disciples—about twelve men. Paul realized that the power of God was not with them. When he asked them if they received the Holy Spirit when they believed, they answered: "No, we have not even heard that there is a Holy Spirit" (Acts 19:2). They received John's baptism but they knew nothing about the Holy Spirit or the Spirit baptism.

We must receive the Spirit baptism after becoming God's children so that we could defeat our enemy, the devil, and overcome all our problems in our lives. Ephesians 5:18 tells us to "not get drunk on wine, which leads to debauchery [but to] be filled with the Spirit."

When we're filled with the Holy Spirit, we can have confidence in our faith. Only then we can receive the power of the Word in us, living a fruit-bearing life.

Years ago, when I went to Germany to preach at a retreat for Korean students in Europe, I visited Kölner Dom (Cologne Cathedral). The construction of Cologne Cathedral began in 1248 but was halted. Work restarted and the edifice was completed to its original Medieval plan in 1880, 632 years after construction had begun. The cathedral is the largest Gothic church in Northern Europe, where thousands of people used to gather and worship God. However, the Cathedral has become more of a tourist attraction and heritage site than a place of worship. This happens because the Holy Spirit is absent. The revival of the church begins with the work of the Holy Spirit. We must receive power and become the witnesses of the gospel of Jesus through the Holy Spirit.

Acts 1:8 says: "But you will receive power when the Holy Spirit comes on you; and you will be my witnesses in Jerusalem, and in all Judea and Samaria, and to the ends of the earth." So be filled with the Holy Spirit and become people of the Spirit so that God can use you as the witnesses of the gospel until Jesus comes again.

2. We must witness Jesus Christ alone.

Apostle Paul explained to those twelve disciples about Jesus: the one John the Baptist talked about was Jesus. In other words, the one who was coming after John the Baptist was Jesus.

Acts 19:4-5 says: "Paul said, 'John's baptism was a baptism of repentance. He told the people to believe in the one coming after him, that is, in Jesus.' On hearing this, they were baptized in the name of the Lord Jesus."

The disciples in Ephesus didn't know anything about the Holy Spirit. After teaching them about the Holy Spirit, Paul baptized them in the name of the Lord Jesus. When Paul placed his hands on them, the Holy Spirit came on them. Acts 19:6-7 says: "When Paul placed his hands on them, the Holy Spirit came on them, and they spoke in tongues and prophesied. There were about twelve men in all." They hadn't even known that there was a Holy Spirit, but when the Holy Spirit came on them, they spoke in tongues and prophesied.

Like this, when we're filled with the Holy Spirit, the Spirit who is within us will help us testify of Jesus. We'll be filled with the Spirit and thus will testify of the thoughts and will of Jesus Christ.

In John 15:26, Jesus said: "When the Advocate comes, whom I will send to you from the Father—the Spirit of truth who goes out from the Father—he will testify of me." The Holy Spirit came to us as the Spirit of truth, helping us to understand the teachings of Jesus and to fulfill the tasks that Jesus entrusted to us.

When we're filled with the Holy Spirit, we'll become like Jesus, bearing the fruit of the Holy Spirit. Galatians 5:22-23 says: "But the fruit of the Spirit is love, joy, peace, forbearance, kindness, goodness, faithfulness, gentleness and self-control. Against such things there is no law." The Holy Spirit will transform us into little Jesuses so that we can exalt Him through our lives and give glory to Him. Since the Holy Spirit is the Spirit of Jesus, when the Holy Spirit comes, we'll be filled with the Spirit of Jesus and therefore, we'll testify of Jesus. We'll boast about Him and exalt Him. We'll become like Jesus.

Be filled with the Holy Spirit and testify of Jesus Christ alone.

3. We must lead the revival.

Acts 19:10 says: "This went on for two years, so that all the Jews and Greeks who lived in the province of Asia heard the word of the Lord."

Paul and the disciples had discussions daily in the lecture hall of Tyrannus for two years, preaching the gospel of Jesus. Then there happened a great revival and as its consequence, the gospel was widely spread from Ephesus to almost all of Asia Minor.

More work of the Holy Spirit was done in Ephesus. Acts 19:11-12 says that "God did extraordinary miracles through Paul, so that even handkerchiefs and aprons that had touched him were taken to the sick, and their illnesses were cured and the evil spirits left them." God performed extraordinary and miraculous healing through Paul.

Some Jews who went around driving out evil spirits tried to invoke the name of the Lord Jesus over those who were demon-possessed. They would say, "In the name of the Jesus whom Paul preaches, I command you to come out." However, one day, a man with the evil spirit jumped on them and overpowered them all. He gave them such a beating that they ran out of the house naked and bleeding.

When this became known to people living in Ephesus, they were terrified, and the name of the Lord Jesus was held in high honor. Many of those who believed came and openly confessed what they had done. Those who had practiced sorcery brought their scrolls together and burned them publicly.

Acts 19:19 says: "A number who had practiced sorcery brought their scrolls together and burned them publicly. When they calculated the value of the scrolls, the total came to fifty thousand drachmas." Fifty thousand drachmas is equivalent to four million US dollars in today's currency. When the Holy Spirit was upon them, the gospel covered the city, which had been filled with idol worships and sorceries. Revival and miracles happened. The power of darkness was expelled. Acts 19:20 says that "in this way the word of the Lord spread widely and grew in power."

Apostle Paul was the main character who preached the gospel and led the revival in this scene of the work of the Holy Spirit. The same things can happen to us. When we're renewed by being filled with the Holy Spirit, God will perform great miracles through us. We can also manifest His glory all around the world. Therefore be seized by the Holy Spirit and as the main characters of the great revival, write the new history of the Holy Spirit.

When the Holy Spirit comes on us, our inner self will be strengthened. All our problems will be resolved. Let's become like Jesus and serve the impoverished and the neglected with the love of Jesus. We'll become the witnesses of the gospel with the Spirit. So, be filled with the Holy Spirit and live victoriously in the Lord, testify of Jesus until He comes again. As the great and faithful servants of God, continue doing His work mentioned in Acts.

Pastor Yong-Won Shin, Chairperson of the Rehabilitation Community for the Drug-addict

Yong-Won Shin lost his father when he was nine, and his poor mother raised him all by herself. He was very smart and wanted to become a lawyer. But when he was 18, he overheard one of his friend's mother, saying: "don't hang out with someone like Yong-Won, poor and fatherless."

These words broke his heart and he started walking the wrong path. He hung out with gangs. When he was forced to join the military, he cut his left index finger and was dishonorably discharged from the military.

He made millions of dollars by facilitating moneylending business, real estate auctions and casinos. His golden days did not last long, though. He started drugs. He sniffed glue, abused pain killers, smoked marijuana and injected methamphetamine.

He was placed on the wanted list for a violent criminal event in 1994. In 1998, he was hiding in a small prayer house and decided that he would rather die. He was about to hang himself when he remembered his faithful Christian mother's proverb: "man cannot live without the grace of God." He went into a closet in the prayer house and cried out to God. Then fire fell on him! He received the Holy Spirit. Shin said:

> I cried to God, "God, if you are really living, save me, please. If you save me, I will never betray you." Then fire fell on me and I began to speak something I didn't understand. It was at least ten times more entrancing an experience than Philopon. The world looked different and I had new values of life. I wanted to pay my debt to those whose homes and souls had been destroyed because of me.

After receiving the Holy Spirit, he turned himself in to the police and did his time in prison for his crimes. After that, he studied Theology and became a minister. He visited prisons and began to help the prisoners. He became a pastor of a church for the ex-drug-addict. He runs a rice cake factory called the Five Loaves of Bread, where ex-convicts make and sell rice cakes. He helps those battling addiction and tries to heal them spiritually and physically.

Shin said: "I am renewed by being filled with the Holy spirit. My goal of life is to live for God. Jesus stayed with the orphans, widows, and the sick. I also want to work for the disadvantaged."

When we are filled with the Holy Spirit, we'll be clothed in the new self and our old selves will disappear. Those who are renewed by being filled with the Holy Spirit will preach the gospel and take the lead in the work of revival.

4

Following Jesus: Spirituality of Disciples

The spirituality of prayer

10. A Great Mother

11. Have Mercy on Me

12. The Grace at the Ford of the Jabbok

10

A Great Mother

> *In her deep anguish Hannah prayed to the Lord, weeping bitterly. And she made a vow, saying, "Lord Almighty, if you will only look on your servant's misery and remember me, and not forget your servant but give her a son, then I will give him to the Lord for all the days of his life, and no razor will ever be used on his head." As she kept on praying to the Lord, Eli observed her mouth. Hannah was praying in her heart, and her lips were moving but her voice was not heard. Eli thought she was drunk.* (1 Samuel 1:10-13)

God has given us many gifts and one of the greatest is mothers. We exist because we have our mothers. St. Augustine, one of the most important Church fathers, John Wesley, the founder of Methodist churches, and Abraham Lincoln, who carried out the emancipation of slaves, all had faithful mothers who prayed. Great figures in human history came into existence through mothers of prayer.

Samuel was one of the greatest servants and priests of God in the Old Testament, and his mother Hannah was a woman of strong prayer.

1. Hannah devoted herself to prayer.

During the period of Biblical judges, there was a man named Elkanah. He had two wives, Hannah and Peninnah. Peninnah had children but Hannah had none. Since Hannah was childless for a long time, she was deeply troubled even though Elkanah loved her more than he loved Peninnah. So Peninnah kept provoking Hannah until she wept and wouldn't eat. Even though she was deeply saddened, Hannah didn't want to solve this problem by fighting. Instead, she went up to the temple of God and prayed to the Lord, pouring out her heart to Him and weeping bitterly.

1 Samuel 1:10 says: "In her deep anguish Hannah prayed to the Lord, weeping bitterly."

When we encounter problems or difficulties, we must come to the Lord, our problem solver, by ardently praying to Him and weeping. When we pray with tears, God hears our prayers and answers them. Psalm 126:5 says that "those who sow with tears will reap with songs of joy." Our teardrops will turn into joy and we'll receive God's grace and blessings through our tearful prayers.

Hannah made a vow when she prayed. 1 Samuel 1:11 says:

And she made a vow, saying, "Lord Almighty, if you will only look on your servant's misery and remember me, and not forget your servant but give her a son, then I will give him to the Lord for all the days of his life, and no razor will ever be used on his head."

Hannah made a vow to give her son to the Lord as a Nazirite throughout his life if He gave her a son. A Nazirite is someone who sanctifies himself and gives his whole life to the Lord. By making this vow, Hannah sought God's will before she sought her own. We, too, must pray to God and seek His glory.

Hannah consistently prayed with patience. 1 Samuel 1:12-13 says: "As she kept on praying to the Lord, Eli observed her mouth. Hannah was praying in her heart, and her lips were moving but her voice was not heard. Eli thought she was drunk." She prayed with all her might for so long that she couldn't say her prayer audibly. Her lips were moving but her voice wasn't heard. She prayed with all her strength until God would answer her prayer. Isaiah 58:9 says: "Then you will call, and the Lord will answer; you will cry for help, and he will say: Here am I." When we cry out to the Lord persistently and patiently, the Lord will answer our prayers.

Like in Hannah's case, the prayer of a mother changes her children's destiny. Patiently pray for your children with faith, wholeheartedly weeping for them.

2. Hannah had positive faith.

1 Samuel 1:17-18 says: "Eli answered, 'Go in peace, and may the God of Israel grant you what you have asked of him.' She said, 'May your servant find favor in your eyes.' Then she went her way and ate something, and her face was no longer downcast."

Eli was impressed by Hannah's fervent prayer so much that he blessed her saying, "Go in peace, and may the God of Israel grant you what you have asked of Him" (verse 17). At that moment, she found peace. She went back home with joy and thanksgiving. She didn't worry anymore. Her face was no longer downcast. She accepted the word of Eli the priest as God's and believed that He would grant a son to her. Even though nothing seemed to have changed, Hannah was confident that God answered her prayer.

Like Hannah, we shouldn't doubt after praying. We must have confidence in the Lord. Jesus said in Matthew 21:22: "If you believe, you will receive whatever you ask for in prayer."

Why did all the adult male Israelites, who were twenty years or older, die in the desert except Joshua and Caleb? Why couldn't they enter the promised land after they'd come out of Egypt? That was because only Joshua and Caleb trusted God, marching forward with positive faith. The rest didn't trust God but complained and grumbled so they couldn't enjoy the fulfillment of His promise.

James 1:6-7 says: "But when you ask, you must believe and not doubt, because the one who doubts is like a wave of the sea, blown and tossed by the wind. That person should not expect to receive anything from the Lord." God blesses those who believe

His Word of promises and accept it with faith. He doesn't bless us if we doubt His Word. We can only experience His miracles when we march forward with positive faith.

Don't give up even when you are surrounded by various problems or difficulties. Experience God's wonderful miracles by trusting His Word and by marching forward with absolute, positive faith.

3. Hannah had the faith of total dedication.

1 Samuel 1:27-28 says: "'I prayed for this child, and the Lord has granted me what I asked of him. So now I give him to the Lord. For his whole life he will be given over to the Lord.' And he worshiped the Lord there." Hannah gave Samuel to God just as she said she would. Even though he was the son that she had longed to have for a very long time, she didn't forget her vow to God.

Many people pray to God when they're troubled, saying, "Lord, if you answer my prayer, I will do such and such things for you." But, when God answers their prayers, they renege on their promises.

1 Samuel 2:21 says: "And the Lord was gracious to Hannah;

she gave birth to three sons and two daughters. Meanwhile, the boy Samuel grew up in the presence of the Lord." When we dedicate ourselves to the Lord, He will bless us even more. Hannah didn't forget the grace that God gave her. She lived a life of dedication with joy and thanksgiving. God saw her faith and gave her three more sons and two daughters.

Most people are accustomed to receiving but are very stingy about giving. How much blessing we have received from God! Yet we're reluctant to give something back to Him or to share with our neighbors. We need to dedicate ourselves to Him and follow His commandment: love God and love people. When we serve others, God will open the floodgates of heaven and pour bountiful blessings. Have holy dreams and give glory to God by devoting yourself to the Lord and by serving your neighbors.

Pray to God with all your might in the same way as Hannah did. March forward with positive faith. Emulate His love with your sacrificial love for your neighbors. May you be parents of great faith who change their home into a blessed place and lead their children to God in this era of confusion, in which the moral standard collapsed.

11

Have Mercy on Me

Then they came to Jericho. As Jesus and his disciples, together with a large crowd, were leaving the city, a blind man, Bartimaeus (which means "son of Timaeus"), was sitting by the roadside begging. When he heard that it was Jesus of Nazareth, he began to shout, "Jesus, Son of David, have mercy on me!" Many rebuked him and told him to be quiet, but he shouted all the more, "Son of David, have mercy on me!" Jesus stopped and said, "Call him." So they called to the blind man, "Cheer up! On your feet! He's calling you." Throwing his cloak aside, he jumped to his feet and came to Jesus. "What do you want me to do for you?" Jesus asked him. The blind man said, "Rabbi, I want to see." "Go," said Jesus, "your faith has healed you." Immediately he received his sight and followed Jesus along the road. (Mark 10:46-52)

People think the world revolves around them. They're likely to either be prideful or fall into inferiority. We need to have a correct self-identity in God. We're His blessed children and He loves us so greatly. He makes all things work together for our good and uses us for His glory. We must give up our own standards and look at all things from God's perspective, seeking the grace and mercy from the Lord.

When God has mercy on us, we're healed from disabilities and sicknesses that negatively affect us physically, mentally, and spiritually. We'll enjoy the marvelous grace and peace in Him.

God's grace is prevalent in the story of Bartimaeus. Bartimaeus was born blind but he received his sight when Jesus had mercy on him. Then he began a new life of faith.

1. The life with physical blindness

Mark 10:46 says: "Then they came to Jericho. As Jesus and his disciples, together with a large crowd, were leaving the city, a blind man, Bartimaeus (which means 'son of Timaeus'), was sitting by the roadside begging." Jesus was passing by Jericho on His way to Jerusalem, where He was going to be crucified. A large crowd was following Him and there was Bartimaeus, a blind man, who was sitting by the roadside begging.

It was 2,000 years ago and the only thing the blind man could do was to be a mendicant. No one helped him and he was hopeless due to his physical disability.

Even today people live with disabilities—big or small. But we shouldn't be frustrated or be disheartened because Jesus turned all our despair, disabilities, and diseases into healing, recovery, and hope on the cross 2,000 years ago. We were healed from all our infirmities 2,000 years ago through His death on the cross.

We know very well that Jesus healed all those who came to Him with various diseases during His public ministry. Matthew 4:23-24 says:

> Jesus went throughout Galilee, teaching in their synagogues, proclaiming the good news of the kingdom, and healing every disease and sickness among the people. News about him spread all over Syria, and people brought to him all who were ill with various diseases, those suffering severe

pain, the demon-possessed, those having seizures, and the paralyzed; and he healed them.

Jesus the merciful healer from 2000 years ago is still with us right now, so don't worry if you have disabilities or diseases. Experience the amazing grace of healing and recovery of God by looking to Jesus who is the same yesterday, today, and forever.

2. The life with mental blindness

A physical disability greatly affects the life and personality of the person with a disability, which often extends to his disability at heart. He's likely to be irascible, pessimistic or violent.

The man who was lying at the pool called Bethesda was exactly the person described above. He had been an invalid for thirty-eight years. Jesus saw him lying there and asked him, "Do you want to get well?" (John 5:6). Instead of saying, "Yes, Sir," right away, he complained, saying, "Sir … I have no one to help me into the pool when the water is stirred. While I am trying to get in, someone else goes down ahead of me" (John 5:7). Even though Jesus the Healer was speaking to him, he complained. He had a more serious disability, a broken heart, than he had on his body.

Many people these days suffer from mental illnesses due to many factors, including, but not limited to, worrying about the future, feeling empty, and relational problems. Those who can't look beyond their limited perspective become overly sensitive and pessimistic. Jesus frees us from these dark thoughts. Trust in Jesus with an active and positive mind!

When Bartimaeus heard that Jesus was passing, he began to shout. Mark 10:47 says that "when he heard that it was Jesus of Nazareth, he began to shout, 'Jesus, Son of David, have mercy on me!'" But people excoriated him and told him to be quiet. Instead of listening to the people, Bartimaeus "shouted all the more, 'Son of David, have mercy on me!'" (Mark 10:48). Regardless of people's contempt and rebuke, he continued to shout, asking Jesus' mercy.

People often rebuke us when we desperately cry out to Jesus. They may hate us but remember: Jesus always listens to our prayers. So don't listen to the voices of the world that put you down. Shout even more, looking to Jesus who is there to listen. The Lord will have mercy on you, surely pouring out His blessings and miracles.

3. The life with spiritual blindness

Who are the true blind? Those who don't believe in Jesus. Since their spirits are dead, they can't enjoy spiritual blessings. But thank God, because there's a way for them to be restored and rescued from spiritual blindness. Anyone can be born again and be adopted by God when he or she puts his or her faith in Jesus.

John 1:12 says: "Yet to all who did receive him, to those who believed in his name, he gave the right to become children of God." Our status changes the moment we repent. Starting from that point, we will begin a new life as His children.

Bartimaeus threw his cloak aside, jumped to his feet, and came to Jesus when Jesus called him (Mark 10:50). When Jesus asked, "what do you want me to do for you?" he said without delay, "Rabbi, I want to see" (Mark 10:51).

Of course, Jesus knew what the blind man wanted, but He wanted to hear it from him—the confession of his faith on his lips. When Bartimaeus proclaimed his faith, something wonderful happened: "He received his sight and followed Jesus along the road" (Mark 10:52).

Jesus saw that Bartimaeus had a steadfast faith and healed him. His faith healed him! Bartimaeus then followed Jesus along the road because Bartimaeus' physical eyes and spiritual eyes were opened.

Jesus is asking the same question to you: "What do you want me to do for you?" Earnestly cry out to Him again and again with strong and bold faith. Cry out to the Lord for healing your physical diseases and spiritual wounds. When we earnestly cry out to Him, Jesus will have mercy on us and surely answer our prayers.

12

The Grace at the Ford of the Jabbok

So Jacob was left alone, and a man wrestled with him till daybreak. When the man saw that he could not overpower him, he touched the socket of Jacob's hip so that his hip was wrenched as he wrestled with the man. Then the man said, "Let me go, for it is daybreak." But Jacob replied, "I will not let you go unless you bless me." The man asked him, "What is your name?" "Jacob," he answered. Then the man said, "Your name will no longer be Jacob, but Israel, because you have struggled with God and with humans and have overcome." Jacob said, "Please tell me your name." But he replied, "Why do you ask my name?" Then he blessed him there. (Genesis 32:24-29)

There's no one that doesn't go through any suffering at all in his or her entire life. Everybody goes through some sufferings—big or small. To Christians, suffering is a process for greater blessings.

Scripture doesn't tell us that suffering is a curse or evidence that we're forsaken by God. It tells us that suffering is rather like an overture which brings God's blessings to us.

God wants us to live righteously, which requires that we go through trials to enjoy true peace. He constantly sanctifies us so that we may understand and pursue His heart. The people that God used suffered but overcame them successfully. Jacob fervently prayed during times of hardship and God transformed him into a new person at the Ford of the Jabbok.

1. A river that is lying before us

Jacob deceived his twin brother Esau and stole the firstborn's blessing, so he had to flee from his brother and live in his uncle Laban's house. Twenty years later, he left his uncle's house to come back home, bringing his wives, children, and a large flock of his livestock and the goods he had accumulated. But trouble was waiting for him: Esau, who'd been waiting for revenge ever since Jacob fled, was coming to meet him with four hundred men.

Frightened, Jacob planned to avoid Esau's attack. He brought more than a total of 550 animals—cows, goats, rams, and other goods for Esau to pacify his brother. But he was still fearful so he got up at night and sent his family to cross the Ford of the Jabbok. After that, he sent over all his possessions. So Jacob was left alone; neither his wealth nor family could protect him from the threat of Esau. This was why Jacob couldn't cross the Ford of the Jabbok.

What kind of ford is lying in front of you? What hinders or haunts you from marching forward? Is it broken familial relationships? Betrayal? Conflicts between labor and management? Whatever it may be, we must cross these fords of conflicts. But we can't cross with our own strength; we need help, and only Jesus can help us.

Jesus not only stays with us always, but He also intercedes for us always. He alone can put an end to all conflicts, heal relationships, and help us live harmoniously. So listen to His voice and accept His invitation.

Jesus said in Matthew 11:29: "Take my yoke upon you and

learn from me, for I am gentle and humble in heart, and you will find rest for your souls." Come to the Lord. Leave all your burdens at the cross. He'll help us cross that impossible ford and give us true peace and rest.

2. When our ego gets broken

Jacob met an angel of God while he was alone at the Ford of the Jabbok. So, Jacob clung to the angel and didn't let him go. He prayed hard, risking his life.

The angel wrestled with Jacob until daybreak. When the angel saw that he couldn't overpower Jacob, he touched the socket of Jacob's hip so that Jacob's hip was wrenched. Jacob had to limp for the rest of his life. He couldn't run away from Esau even if he wanted to.

However, this incident became the turning point of Jacob's life. God broke Jacob's ego as well as his hip socket. Jacob used to be cunning and greedy, lying and deceiving others to achieve his goal. He used to live in accordance with his own desires and will. So God broke Jacob's self-oriented ego.

Now that Jacob was broken and made low, he clung to God. Genesis 32:26 says: "Then the man said, 'Let me go, for it is daybreak.' But Jacob replied, 'I will not let you go unless you bless me.'"

Jacob didn't let go of the angel of God and asked for blessing. Jacob had nothing there with him—no wife, no children, no wealth, and no health. He had no one but God.

Totally broken and made low at the Ford of the Jabbok, Jacob began a new life as a man of faith and trusted God alone. He realized that he couldn't live without the help from God. Indeed, the Lord is our only hope in the course of our life.

Why is suffering a blessing? Because our pride is totally broken. We used to trust in our own strength, education, background, or possessions. But, when we're humbled, we turn into the men and women of faith. So we must be broken before the Lord. God blesses us only when we look to Him and trust in Him alone.

3. The life in which God reigns

The angel of God asked Jacob what his name was. In those days, one's name indicated his or her status and identity. "Jacob" means "he grasps the heel," a Hebrew idiom for "he deceives," and Jacob lived the life exactly as what his name meant.

But Genesis 32:28 says: "Then the man said, 'Your name will no longer be Jacob, but Israel, because you have struggled with God and with humans and have overcome.'" The angel told Jacob that his name would no longer be Jacob. By doing so, God erased all the shameful memories of Jacob's past. God gave him a new name, Israel, through His angel. Now Jacob obtained a new identity and status. Israel means "he struggles with God," "God reigns," "God heals" or "God judges."

God was going to reign over Jacob's life. Jacob used to live like a swindler before, but he could live a blessed life over which God reigns. Jacob met God!

Genesis 32:31 says: "The sun rose above him as he passed Peniel, and he was limping because of his hip." The sun rose after the angel gave Jacob a new name. In the same way, after we meet God in the night of suffering, the sun of hope will rise.

Even though Jacob limped the rest of his life, he began a new life. What's more amazing is that Esau's mind also changed: he felt sorry for Jacob when he saw Jacob haggardly approaching him. His heart melted when he saw his twin brother.

When the Lord is with us, our enemies will turn into our friends. Hatred will turn into forgiveness. Fights will turn into love. We may have been lowly and obscure but we will become the great servants of God. Pray for that grand turning point under the cross. Live as the great people of God in whom He dwells.

Elder Eung-Sun Kim

Elder Seung-Kyu Kim was the former Director of the National Intelligence Service. His family is a Christian family for five generations. More than 100 family members get together to worship God at the end or the beginning of a year. They get together in memory of their parents Elder Eung-Sun Kim and Senior Deaconess Yeo-Ok Park.

Eung-Sun Kim had nine children. He had a strict rule to start a day with prayer. So he would wake up all his children early in the morning and worshipped God at home before setting out to church for early morning prayer meetings.

One cold winter day, Elder and Mrs. Kim left home to go to church for early morning prayer but they came back home thoroughly drenched. They slipped on ice and fell into a creek. It was so cold that icicles were hanging down from their clothes. They just changed their clothes and went to church without trying to warm up themselves.

Even though he was poor, he started a day with prayer and planted strong faith in the hearts of his children at their early age through early morning prayers and home worships. His children became successful. They became the leaders of Korea—the Director of NIS, a cabinet member, a congressman, a school principal, and a CEO of an enterprise. The nine children of Elder Kim gave birth to 104 grandchildren to Elder Kim—all faithful Christians. There are 16 elders and senior deaconesses. Watching their parents praying and reading the Bible all the time, Kim's offspring established a great family of faith.

5

Following Jesus: Spirituality of Disciples

The spirituality of absolute, positive faith

13. Be Strong and Courageous

14. Faith That Makes Impossible Things Possible

15. Quiet! Be Still!

13

Be Strong and Courageous

> *Be strong and courageous. Do not be afraid or terrified because of them, for the Lord your God goes with you; he will never leave you nor forsake you." Then Moses summoned Joshua and said to him in the presence of all Israel, "Be strong and courageous, for you must go with this people into the land that the Lord swore to their ancestors to give them, and you must divide it among them as their inheritance. The Lord himself goes before you and will be with you; he will never leave you nor forsake you. Do not be afraid; do not be discouraged."* (Deuteronomy 31:6-8)

We feel very insecure about our future. We feel hopeless when we face unexpected problems. But the Bible tells us to be strong and courageous. As God's precious servants, we need to overcome all our issues and live victoriously by trusting in God.

1. We must have strong faith.

Moses knew that he had finished his work and that God would call him up soon. But he was worried about the Israelites since they would have to fight the Canaanites, who were of great size, mighty in battle with chariots fitted with iron. Moses was worried that the Israelites would become fearful even before fighting the Canaanites.

Inspired by the God of grace, Moses told Joshua, his successor, and the Israelites: "Be strong and courageous. Do not be afraid or terrified because of them, for the Lord your God goes with you; he will never leave you nor forsake you" (Deuteronomy 31:6). God also told Joshua through Moses to be strong and courageous three times in Joshua 1:6-9.

Proverbs 4:23 tells us to "guard [our] heart[s], for everything [we] do flows from it." We must guard our hearts. When our hearts collapse, everything also collapses. This is why Moses repeatedly exhorted Joshua and the whole Israel community to be strong and courageous. When we look at ourselves or other people, we're bound to crumble. So we shouldn't look at our surroundings. We must march forward and fix eyes on Jesus, the pioneer and perfecter of our faith.

In John 16:33, Jesus says: "I have told you these things, so that in me you may have peace. In this world you will have trouble. But take heart! I have overcome the world." The Lord Jesus who has overcome the world is with us. We have nothing to worry about and we don't need to feel insecure or anxious. God will help us if we march forward with faith in Jesus alone, trusting in Him even when we're surrounded by difficulties.

2. We must become the servants of God.

Deuteronomy 31:6b says: "For the Lord your God goes with you; he will never leave you nor forsake you." When we're assured that God is with us, we can overcome anything. We can be strong and courageous, knowing that God will never leave us or forsake us.

Matthew 28:20b says: "And surely I am with you always, to

the very end of the age." Hebrews 13:5b also says, "Never will I leave you; never will I forsake you."

God is with us. Jesus is with us. The Holy Spirit is always with us. Therefore, we must march forward, believing and trusting in God of Immanuel.

Psalm 23:1-2 says: "The Lord is my shepherd, I lack nothing. He makes me lie down in green pastures, he leads me beside quiet waters." Things of this world may momentarily please us, but nothing could fully quench the fundamental thirst of our soul.

Peace and rest in God can't be compared with anything in the world. When we receive the Lord Jesus into our hearts, God will become our shepherd and lead our ways. As His good and faithful servants, we should always talk to Him. Be like Joshua, strong and courageous, and accomplish God's will by holding onto His promises.

3. We must become the leaders who fulfill the promises of the Word.

Deuteronomy 31:7 says:

Then Moses summoned Joshua and said to him in the presence of all Israel, "Be strong and courageous, for you must go with this people into the land that the Lord swore to their ancestors to give them, and you must divide it among them as their inheritance."

This verse is closely related to Genesis 12:1 which God promised Abram (Abraham), his son Isaac, and his grandson Jacob. It says: "The Lord had said to Abram, 'Go from your country, your people and your father's household to the land I will show you.'"

This promise of God extended to Isaac, Abraham's son. Genesis 26:2-4 says:

The Lord appeared to Isaac and said, "Do not go down to Egypt; live in the land where I tell you to live. Stay in this land for a while, and I will be with you and will bless you. For to you and your descendants I will give all these lands and will confirm the oath I swore to your father Abraham. I will make your descendants as numerous as the stars in the sky and will give them all these lands, and through your offspring all nations on earth will be blessed."

Genesis 28:13-14 says:

There above it stood the Lord, and he said: "I am the Lord, the God of your father Abraham and the God of Isaac. I will give you and your descendants the land on which you are lying. Your descendants will be like the dust of the earth, and you will spread out to the west and to the east, to the north and to the south. All peoples on earth will be blessed through you and your offspring."

This promise extended from Isaac to his son Jacob. They all received the word of God's promise and trusted it. They faced problems, but by His grace, God always let them come back to Canaan. God never changes and certainly fulfills His promise.

Therefore, we must become great leaders in this world by firmly trusting in God's words. As people of faith, we must overcome all our tribulations by walking with the Lord. We must set a fine example of faith in believing and accomplishing the Word of God. Then all those who see us and our offspring will be blessed by God.

This world is calling us for help. Those who are in deep distress are calling us. Those who are badly hurt and wounded are calling us too. We need to hear their cries for help and go to them.

As precious servants of God, we must go to them with strong and courageous faith, showing the love of Jesus to them, giving them strength and courage, and accomplishing the great works of God.

Be the strong and courageous children of God, obeying His word and accomplishing it.

14

Faith That Makes Impossible Things Possible

A few days later, when Jesus again entered Capernaum, the people heard that he had come home. They gathered in such large numbers that there was no room left, not even outside the door, and he preached the word to them. Some men came, bringing to him a paralyzed man, carried by four of them. Since they could not get him to Jesus because of the crowd, they made an opening in the roof above Jesus by digging through it and then lowered the mat the man was lying on. When Jesus saw their faith, he said to the paralyzed man, "Son, your sins are forgiven." (Mark 2:1-5)

Christian life starts with faith in Jesus. We can't claim to be Christians without faith because the foundation of our faith is

Jesus. Hebrews 12:2 says that we must "fix [our] eyes on Jesus, the pioneer and perfecter of faith." We must always look to the Lord Jesus in our Christian life. If we have true faith, we put down everything we have and believe in God alone with total trust.

Even though Abraham made many mistakes, God saw his faith and chose him, making him the father of faith. So live the life of faith and please Him. Let's see how people of faith experienced God's miracles.

1. Obstacles that lay ahead of us

Mark 2:2 says: "They gathered in such large numbers that there was no room left, not even outside the door, and he preached the word to them."

Jesus went to a house in Capernaum and preached the Word. When people heard that Jesus was in Capernaum, so many people showed up that there was no room left, not even outside the door. Since Jesus' words were full of God's grace, a large crowd gathered, admiring the Word.

There was a paralyzed man in town. He couldn't move at all, so his four friends carried him on a mat and brought him to the house where Jesus was preaching. His friends did so because they heard that Jesus was the Messiah, the Son of God, who healed all diseases and raised the dead.

Even today, there isn't a problem that Jesus can't solve or a disease that Jesus can't heal. He's the God of miracles, healing and forgiveness.

The four friends couldn't get him to Jesus because of the large crowd. There was an obstacle that was keeping them from taking their friend to Jesus. In the same way, there is an obstacle between God and us—sin. We've become paralyzed due to sin and unable to come to Jesus. But God chose and called us by His absolute grace.

Even though there was an obstacle, the four friends of the paralytic didn't give up or go back. They didn't concentrate on the obstacle, but looked for a way to come to Jesus with eyes of faith. Their eyes of faith opened and found a way. They said, "There is a way. Let's go up to the roof and make an opening in the roof." Faith gives rise to miracles. It makes impossible things possible.

When we serve the Lord, we often have obstacles lying before us. We may encounter problems and difficulties. Even so, we must overcome all our difficulties with faith. No matter what kind of problems or difficulties you may encounter, never give up or step backward but march forward with faith.

2. The work of unity

Mark 2:3 says: "Some men came, bringing to him a paralyzed man, carried by four of them."

The four people brought a paralyzed man to Jesus. Psalm 133:1 says: "How good and pleasant it is when God's people live together in unity!" We must be united. When we're united, a miracle will take place.

In Exodus, while the Israelites fought the Amalekites, Moses, Aaron, and Hur went to the top of the hill. Moses held up his hands and prayed and the Israelites defeated the Amalekites. We must also be united. Our homes, mission groups and workplaces should be united. All the church departments must be united and so should the whole country.

Acts 2:44-47 says:

> All the believers were together and had everything in common. They sold property and possessions to give to anyone who had need. Every day they continued to meet together in the temple courts. They broke bread in their homes and ate together with glad and sincere hearts, praising God and enjoying the favor of all the people. And the Lord added to their number daily those who were being saved.

The early Christian community formed the unity of love in the church. There was no poor person in the church. When someone poor came to church, people supported him or her. When the church was united with God's love, many people enjoyed great revival and growth.

But we can't form unity with our own strength. We need the grace of the Holy Spirit. Ephesians 4:3 says: "Make every effort to keep the unity of the Spirit through the bond of peace." Instead of looking for the weak points and faults of one another, criticizing and fighting, we must have one heart and do the work that God has entrusted to us, brightening this dark world. Then the blessing that God has prepared for us will be given to us. Our future will be filled with great miracles.

3. Miracles of faith

Mark 2:4-5 says:

> Since they could not get him to Jesus because of the crowd, they made an opening in the roof above Jesus by digging through it and then lowered the mat the man was lying on. When Jesus saw their faith, he said to the paralyzed man, "Son, your sins are forgiven."

In those days, the Palestinian houses had flat roofs. They laid wood panels for the roof and put wood sticks on it, covering them with mud. So it wasn't an impossible thing to dig a hole in the roof. There also were stairs that led to the roof from the ground. Since they had to lower the mat through the hole, with the paralytic on it, they had to dig a large hole.

People rebuked these four men but they didn't care. What they wanted was to lower their paralyzed friend before the Lord Jesus and to get him healed.

If we have faith, we must march forward with our eyes fixed on Jesus. We shouldn't listen to people. They usually try to bring us down and if we listen to them, we can't expect any miracles.

When General MacArthur planned an amphibious landing at Incheon, other generals opposed him because Incheon's natural and artificial defenses were formidable. They pointed out that the current of the channels was dangerously quick and tides were so extreme to prevent immediate follow-on landings. But MacArthur successfully landed at Incheon and produced a sufficiently decisive victory.

Faith makes impossible things possible. Jesus saw the four friends' faith and was quite impressed. He healed the paralyzed man. Mark 2:11-12 says: "'I tell you, get up, take your mat and go home.' He got up, took his mat and walked out in full view of them all. This amazed everyone and they praised God, saying, 'We have never seen anything like this!'"

If we have faith, something like this can happen today too. So never give up. Don't get discouraged even when it seems impossible and hold onto God's promises. March forward with absolute, positive faith.

God is leading your life through the end. Even when you encounter various problems, diseases, or difficulties in your homes, look to Jesus. Miracles will happen to you when you march forward with absolute, positive faith. You will receive God's grace. Your problems will be resolved. Live as the giants of great faith.

15

Quiet! Be Still!

That day when evening came, he said to his disciples, "Let us go over to the other side." Leaving the crowd behind, they took him along, just as he was, in the boat. There were also other boats with him. A furious squall came up, and the waves broke over the boat, so that it was nearly swamped. Jesus was in the stern, sleeping on a cushion. The disciples woke him and said to him, "Teacher, don't you care if we drown?" He got up, rebuked the wind and said to the waves, "Quiet! Be still!" Then the wind died down and it was completely calm. He said to his disciples, "Why are you so afraid? Do you still have no faith?" They were terrified and asked each other, "Who is this? Even the wind and the waves obey him!" (Mark 4:35-41)

Everything in this world is shaking these days. Nation fight against nation, and kingdom against kingdom. There are famines and earthquakes in various places. We can't solve any of these problems alone. We must come to God, our problem solver, and admit our weakness. God will help us when we believe in Him who created the whole universe and who reigns over all things.

1. The disciples met a storm.

Jesus preached all day long and when evening came, He went over to the other side of the Sea of Galilee on a boat. Then, "a furious squall came up, and the waves broke over the boat, so that it was nearly swamped" (Mark 4:37).

In this life, we're also going to encounter unexpected squalls. The doctors may tell you that you have terminal cancer, your company may go bankrupt, or your child may be rebellious. Even when you encounter these storms in life, don't be shaken, for 1 Peter 4:12 tells us to "not be surprised at the fiery ordeal that has come on you to test you, as though something strange were happening to you." A furious squall comes to you because God wants to strengthen your faith through the storm.

He wants your faith to grow.

When we face unexpected issues, we easily become anxious because we concentrate on our problems. But we must focus on Jesus who is far bigger than our problems. Rather than looking at the storms, look to Jesus, our problem solver.

Because we're so quick to get discouraged, we must quickly come to God when we face trials and tribulations. We need to ask God for His mercy and ask Him to rescue us from this place of hopelessness.

2. Jesus was sleeping in the boat.

Mark 4:38 says: "Jesus was in the stern, sleeping on a cushion. The disciples woke him and said to him, 'Teacher, don't you care if we drown?'"

Jesus was sleeping in the middle of the furious storm. Here lies a very important spiritual lesson that we have to learn from: we must always walk with Jesus rather than trying to solve problems on our own and not asking Jesus for help. The disciples tried to balance the boat without Jesus. When they were on the verge of drowning, they go to Jesus, complaining, "Teacher, don't you care if we drown?" (Mark 4:38).

Of course, Jesus cared. The disciples just weren't seeking help from Him until that moment, but Jesus was with them throughout the storm. Psalm 50:15 says: "And call on me in the day of trouble; I will deliver you, and you will honor me." Therefore, we must call on the Lord Jesus who is always with us and ask for His help.

In Matthew 15, there is an episode of a Canaanite woman. She came to Jesus, crying out, "Lord, Son of David, have mercy on me!" (Matthew 15:22). However, Jesus replied coldly, "It is not right to take the children's bread and toss it to the dogs," (Matthew 15:26) and turned away. Even so, she didn't retreat. "Yes it is, Lord," she said, "even the dogs eat the crumbs that fall from their master's table" (Matthew 15:27). Her eagerness even for the crumbs of the grace of God touched Jesus.

Matthew 15:28 says: "Then Jesus said to her, 'Woman, you have great faith! Your request is granted.' And her daughter was healed at that moment."

Seek help from the Lord and cry out to Him like the Canaanite woman did. Then Jesus will grant our requests.

When we pray eagerly, miracles will happen. So don't doubt or retreat but march forward with faith.

3. Jesus calmed the storm.

Mark 4:39 says: "He got up, rebuked the wind and said to the waves, 'Quiet! Be still!' Then the wind died down and it was completely calm." Even if you're facing hardships, proclaim with confidence in Jesus' name and tell the devil to go away. Then the enemy will see that the Spirit is within you and run away.

The most furious storm is the storm in our hearts. Some people even hate their lives due to constant mood swings. We need to bring these stresses to Jesus too. Now that Jesus is by our side, we must become strong. Spiritually speaking, we must defeat the devil by the Word of Jesus Christ. We must proclaim with bold confidence, "I command you in the name of Jesus of Nazareth, waves of problems, be quiet. Storms that bring pain and agony, be still! Power of darkness, go away!"

4. The work of faith

Mark 4:40 says: "He said to his disciples, 'Why are you so afraid? Do you still have no faith?'"

The Israelites escaped Egypt after having been enslaved to the Egyptians for 430 years. They were encamped by the sea and the Egyptians were chasing them. Even though they'd been miraculously released from Egypt, they were still terrified because they focused on their surroundings. They totally forgot God's grace and deliverance and complained to Moses, saying, "was it because there were no graves in Egypt that you brought us to the desert to die?" (Exodus 14:11).

Moses answered with bold faith. He said: "Do not be afraid. Stand firm and you will see the deliverance the Lord will bring you today. The Egyptians you see today you will never see again. The Lord will fight for you; you need only to be still" (Exodus 14:13-14). God was telling them to be still because He would fight for them instead.

Therefore, when a furious storm comes, we must have absolute, positive faith. We must believe that we will conquer all our problems more than satisfactorily and that the miracles of God will take place. Don't get disappointed or retreat. March forward with faith, looking to Jesus.

Proclaim to the waves, "Quiet! Be still!" with absolute, positive faith no matter how big the storm may seem. Then the wind will die down and become calm. The beautiful and perfect will of God alone will be accomplished. Give glory to God by looking to Him alone and by marching forward with faith.

Missionary Stanley Jones

Stanley Jones (b. 1984), also known as the world's greatest missionary, was an American Methodist Christian missionary and theologian. Until the age of 87, he'd continued to live a rigorous and active life as a missionary in India. But in December 1971, when Jones was 87, he suffered a stroke while he was leading the Oklahoma Christian Ashram, which resulted in his physical impairment. He realized that it was time for him to prove what he'd been preaching his whole life; he had to show it in his life even during hardship. He had faith that God's "YES" would sustain him and fill all his need even when life says "NO."

He didn't ask God why this happened; he didn't complain. After some months in rehabilitation hospitals, he returned to India and managed to regain mobility and the ability to preach publicly despite major speech difficulties.

He felt that the year for him was the practical application of all they had been preaching—the year of using his infirmities. When life says "NO," God still says "YES," and such was the affirmation he made in his last book, *The Divine Yes!*, which he finished by dictating onto a tape recorder.

6

Following Jesus: Spirituality of Disciples

The spirituality of service and sharing

16. The Greatest of These Is Love

17. What Should We Do

18. Those Whom God Loves

16

The Greatest of These Is Love

If I speak in the tongues of men or of angels, but do not have love, I am only a resounding gong or a clanging cymbal. If I have the gift of prophecy and can fathom all mysteries and all knowledge, and if I have a faith that can move mountains, but do not have love, I am nothing. If I give all I possess to the poor and give over my body to hardship that I may boast, but do not have love, I gain nothing. Love is patient, love is kind. It does not envy, it does not boast, it is not proud. It does not dishonor others, it is not self-seeking, it is not easily angered, it keeps no record of wrongs. Love does not delight in evil but rejoices with the truth. It always protects, always trusts, always hopes, always perseveres.
(1 Corinthians 13:1-7)

God is love. God loved us so much that He opened the door to salvation for us by sending His one and only Son Jesus to this earth and let Him die on the cross. We must examine ourselves in our daily Christian life and share this love with our neighbors. 1 Corinthians 13 shows us what true love is so that we could share God's grace with others.

1. The gift that has no love

1 Corinthians is a letter that Apostle Paul wrote to the church at Corinth. Various gifts of the Holy Spirit appeared frequently in the church: many people prophesied and spoke in tongues, and there were many miracles. The Holy Spirit gives us various gifts so that we can edify the church and give glory to God. But the Corinthians put too much emphasis on the manifestation of the gift. They became sanctimonious and looked down on those who didn't show gifts of the Spirit. This was causing division among the church, so Paul wrote a letter exhorting them to exercise their gift of the Spirit based on the principle of love.

The Scripture says that no spiritual gift is meaningful if it isn't accompanied by the love of Jesus Christ. Even if we speak in the tongues of men or of angels, without love, we would be nothing but a resounding gong or a clanging cymbal. We wouldn't have any good influence on others. Only the words that contain true love can move other people, giving them comfort and peace. Anything that's done without love reaps nothing.

We find similar characteristics that lack love in the Pharisees. They would stand in the temple and pray, fast twice a week, give tithe offerings, and keep all the Ten Commandments. Even so, Jesus rebuked them for their hypocrisy and called them the brood of vipers because actions that were not accompanied by love could not bear any fruit at all.

The essence of God is love. 1 John 4:8 says that "whoever does not love does not know God, because God is love." 1 John 4:12 also tells us that "no one has ever seen God; but if we love one another, God lives in us and his love is made complete in us." When we do all things with love, we will receive the grace of God. When we do all things with love, God will lead us so that we can be the evidences of His love.

The early Christian church was a community of love in

which no one was poor or needy. It was because those who were materially blessed by God sold their possessions and gave it to the church, taking care of the poor and needy. Acts 2:44-45 says: "All the believers were together and had everything in common. They sold property and possessions to give to anyone who had need." Acts 4:32 also says: "All the believers were one in heart and mind. No one claimed that any of their possessions was their own, but they shared everything they had." Since the early Christian church was filled with the Holy Spirit, they had no greed for wealth or possessions. They looked to Jesus who would certainly come again, striving to share the blessings they received with others.

Therefore, we must practice loving. Everything must be done with love without expecting anything in return. People may forget our actions of love, but God surely remembers and He will reward us in heaven.

2. True love

1 Corinthians 13:4-7 says:

Love is patient, love is kind. It does not envy, it does not boast, it is not proud. It does not dishonor others, it is not self-seeking, it is not easily angered, it keeps no record of wrongs. Love does not delight in evil but rejoices with the truth. It always protects, always trusts, always hopes, always perseveres.

We find 15 characteristics of true love in 1 Corinthians 13:4-7. Notice how a third of these characteristics are related to patience: patient, kind, not easily angered, always protects, and always perseveres. To be patient means to control one's temper and feelings. Since people are unable to control their temper, they easily flare up and make irrational decisions that may hurt others.

Even though Moses was a great leader in the history of Israel, he couldn't enter the promised land because he lost his temper. The Israelites arrived at Kadesh Barnea after wandering around the desert for 40 years. Now there was no water for the community and the people quarreled with Moses, complaining. He was angry at the Israelites who had complained throughout their journey through the desert. Even though God had told him to speak to the rock to pour out its water, he raised his arm and struck the rock twice with his staff. Numbers 20:10-11 says:

> He and Aaron gathered the assembly together in front of the rock and Moses said to them, "Listen, you rebels, must we bring you water out of this rock?" Then Moses raised his arm and struck the rock twice with his staff. Water gushed out, and the community and their livestock drank.

Since Moses and Aaron didn't do what God had told them to do, God said to them: "because you did not trust in me enough to honor me as holy in the sight of the Israelites, you will not bring this community into the land I give them" (Numbers 20:12). Even though Moses was a very humble man, more humble than anyone else was, he couldn't enter the promised land that he had so desperately longed for because he failed to control his temper and got angry.

God is very patient with us. 2 Peter 3:9 says: "The Lord is not slow in keeping his promise, as some understand slowness. Instead he is patient with you, not wanting anyone to perish, but everyone to come to repentance." If God hadn't been patient with man, man would have been demolished a long time ago. The history of mankind would have stopped long ago. Since God is patient with us, we're here today, saved through His love and patience.

True love means patience. We must control our hearts and minds and wait patiently under any circumstances. We should wait for the time of God, for He will surely accomplish His work in His time.

Forgiveness should follow patience. Love and forgiveness can't be separated. Before we were saved by God's grace, we were unforgivable sinners. But through Jesus, we became God's forgiven children. We must emulate Jesus' love for us and forgive others that hurt us too. Jesus spoke about forgiveness when He appeared to His disciples in the evening of His resurrection day. John 20:23 says: "If you forgive anyone's sins, their sins are forgiven; if you do not forgive them, they are not forgiven."

Therefore, don't be chained by pain. We receive God's grace when we forgive. How many times should we forgive, then? Peter once asked Jesus how many times he should forgive those who sinned against him. Jesus answered: "I tell you, not seven times, but seventy-seven times" (Matthew 18:22). In other words, we must forgive them infinitely many times. Since Jesus has forgiven us unconditionally, we can't experience any miracles unless we forgive one another. True forgiveness will lead us to the grace of God.

The conclusion of 1 Corinthians 13 is: "And now these three remain: faith, hope and love. But the greatest of these is love" (1 Corinthians 13:13). Be the embodiment of love. Practice love and forgiveness. Serve others with love so that you can greet Jesus with joy when He calls you home.

17

What Should We Do?

John said to the crowds coming out to be baptized by him, "You brood of vipers! Who warned you to flee from the coming wrath? Produce fruit in keeping with repentance. And do not begin to say to yourselves, 'We have Abraham as our father.' For I tell you that out of these stones God can raise up children for Abraham. The ax is already at the root of the trees, and every tree that does not produce good fruit will be cut down and thrown into the fire." "What should we do then?" the crowd asked. John answered, "Anyone who has two shirts should share with the one who has none, and anyone who has food should do the same." Even tax collectors came to be baptized. "Teacher," they asked, "what should we do?" "Don't collect any more than you are required to," he told them. Then some soldiers asked him, "And what should we do?" He replied, "Don't extort money and don't accuse people falsely—be content with your pay." (Luke 3:7-14)

The greatest miracle, grace, and blessing we can experience is to become God's children through our faith in Jesus. We were once slaves of the devil but our status completely changed when we put our faith in Jesus. We need to thank Him for grace and salvation.

But, to be saved, we need to shift our way of life. God requires that we give up our old selves so that we can live like His children.

1. We must repent.

Luke 3:3 says: "He went into all the country around the Jordan, preaching a baptism of repentance for the forgiveness of sins."

Originally, baptism was an Israelite ceremony where one cleansed his or her body. After the Christian church emerged, it has become one in which believers acknowledge that they're saved by Jesus' blood. Our old selves die when we're dunked into the water and we're born again.

John the Baptist baptized the Israelites who were living

in sin and urged them to prepare for the Messiah. Pharisees, Scribes, teachers of Law and Sadducees kept the Law carefully, fasted twice a week and gave one tenth of their earnings. Outwardly, these religious leaders probably looked very holy. But they were actually corrupt, sinful, greedy, and arrogant—full of evil thoughts. They may have received baptism but it was meaningless as they didn't repent. They didn't repent of their sins nor turn from their sinful life.

John the Baptist rebuked these people in Luke 3:7-8, saying:

> You brood of vipers! Who warned you to flee from the coming wrath? Produce fruit in keeping with repentance. And do not begin to say to yourselves, "We have Abraham as our father." For I tell you that out of these stones God can raise up children for Abraham.

To repent means to change directions from sin to Jesus. We need to turn away from sin and give up our old selves.

2. We must bear good fruit.

Luke 3:9 says that "the ax is already at the root of the trees, and every tree that does not produce good fruit will be cut down and thrown into the fire." The Scripture warns us that if we don't repent or produce good fruit, then we'll be cut off from Jesus, the vine. Before we were saved, we were deep in sin; after repenting, we should become like gentle sheep.

The Great Revival in Pyongyang in 1907 was the greatest awakening in the Korean church history. More than 1,500 people gathered at Jangdaehyun Church in Pyongyang for the ten-day revival meetings. On the evening of January 6, 1907, something miraculous happened. The following is the report of the missionaries:

That night, the Holy Spirit came to us with the wailing sound of repentance of the participants. Elder Sun-Joo Gil stood up and repented in front of people. He said, "I am a sinner like Achan." His friend had asked him to look after his estate and take care of his family when he died. In the process of settling his friend's inheritance, he took some of it (100 won) as his commission.

When Gil, the most respected church leader, publicly repented with tears, the congregation began to do the same, hitting the floor with their fists. They went home very late at night from praying and came back to church early the next morning to pray. This is the beginning of the Korean tradition of early morning prayer.

Missionary Harris reported the fruit of this repentance movement:

> Thousands of people started to learn to read. Drunkards, gamblers, thieves, murderers, and many evil spirit worshippers changed into new people. Schools and hospitals were founded, the status of women improved, and people free from shamanism and idol worship. The revival movement stirred up national consciousness to resist Japan's colonial rule and it became the basis of the independence movement. As a result of the revival movement, Pyongyang, which used to be called as Sodom of Korea, became Jerusalem of the East, blazing with the holiness only in 15 years.

As we see in the Great Revival in Pyongyang, people will

bear beautiful fruit when they repent. So switch your direction and turn to Jesus. Bear good fruits.

3. We must practice love and justice.

When John the Baptist proclaimed the message of repentance and fruit-bearing life, the crowd asked him how. Then John told them to exercise love first. Luke 3:11 says: "John answered, 'Anyone who has two shirts should share with the one who has none, and anyone who has food should do the same.'"

After we receive the grace from God, we must share our blessings with other people. Proverbs 19:17 says: "Whoever is kind to the poor lends to the Lord, and he will reward them for what they have done." When we do good things, God will reward us with His abundant grace.

To bear the fruit of repentance, we must practice justice. Luke 3:12-13 says: "Even tax collectors came to be baptized. 'Teacher,' they asked, 'what should we do?' 'Don't collect any more than you are required to,' he told them."

Israel was ruled by the Roman Empire and the Romans

hired the Jews to collect tax. The Jewish tax collectors collected more than they were required to and kept the excessive tax for themselves. So the Jews considered the tax collectors as thieves or robbers. This was the reason that John told them not to collect more than they were required to do. In other words, John the Baptist didn't tell them to change their jobs but to practice sacrifice and justice in what they were doing.

To produce fruit in keeping with repentance also means to live self-contently. Soldiers also came to John and asked what they had to do. He replied: "Don't extort money and don't accuse people falsely—be content with your pay" (Luke 3:14). The soldiers didn't earn much money so they resorted to threatening people for money, and John told them to be content with their pay. Rather than complaining, we should be content with what we have and serve others by sharing our possessions with them. This is true love and service.

As God's children, we must continually repent and produce fruit. We must also give generously to others, serve them, and share what we have with them. Then the abundant blessing of God will be on us and our offspring. Ask Jesus to help you produce the fruit of repentance.

18

Those Whom God Loves

Then Jesus came from Galilee to the Jordan to be baptized by John. But John tried to deter him, saying, "I need to be baptized by you, and do you come to me?" Jesus replied, "Let it be so now; it is proper for us to do this to fulfill all righteousness." Then John consented. As soon as Jesus was baptized, he went up out of the water. At that moment heaven was opened, and he saw the Spirit of God descending like a dove and alighting on him. And a voice from heaven said, "This is my Son, whom I love; with him I am well pleased." (Matthew 3:13-17)

Many people are aimlessly wandering and have no clear goal or direction in their lives, living as wind blows or at the mercy of the waves. How wonderful is God's grace that He chose us and adopted us as His children! He loves us so much that He sent His one and only Son and sacrificed Him for us. Now that He has saved us—unforgivable sinners, we must rejoice in this grace and give endless thanks to Him.

There are a few spiritual lessons to be learned from the scene of Jesus' baptism

1. We must be humble and obedient.

Matthew 3:13-15 says:

Then Jesus came from Galilee to the Jordan to be baptized by John. But John tried to deter him, saying, "I need to be baptized by you, and do you come to me?" Jesus replied, "Let it be so now; it is proper for us to do this to fulfill all righteousness." Then John consented.

When Jesus came to the Jordan to be baptized by John, the latter stated that he should be the one getting baptized by the former, not vice versa.

But John tried to deter Him, saying, "I give baptism of repentance. Are you not the Messiah? It is I who should be baptized by you." Then Jesus replied: "Let it be so now; it is proper for us to do this to fulfill all righteousness" (Matthew 3:15). Jesus came to this earth in exactly the same form as all humans to serve the impoverished, the poorly clothed, the sick, and the hurt. To emphasize this, He was baptized in the same way as other people.

The life of Jesus can be characterized by obedience and humility. Philippians 2:6-8 says:

> Who, being in very nature God, did not consider equality with God something to be used to his own advantage; rather, he made himself nothing by taking the very nature of a servant, being made in human likeness. And being found in appearance as a man, he humbled himself by becoming obedient to death—even death on a cross!

Mark 10:45 also says: "For even the Son of Man did not come to be served, but to serve, and to give his life as a ransom for many."

Jesus was obedient to God's will even to death. The final lesson that He gave to His disciples was service. During the Last Supper Jesus took off His outer clothing, wrapped a towel around His waist, and washed His disciples' feet. John 13:14-15 says: "Now that I, your Lord and Teacher, have washed your feet, you also should wash one another's feet. I have set you an example that you should do as I have done for you."

Therefore, to serve means to wash dirty parts of other people. If we try to show off while claiming to be serving God, it means nothing. We need to praise our Lord God alone with humble hearts. Ask God to help you become His precious servant so that you could give glory to Him and serve others.

2. We must be filled with the Holy Spirit.

Matthew 3:16 says: "As soon as Jesus was baptized, he went up out of the water. At that moment heaven was opened, and he saw the Spirit of God descending like a dove and alighting on him."

Jesus walked with the Holy Spirit throughout His life; He was conceived by the Holy Spirit. Luke 1:35 says: "The angel answered, 'The Holy Spirit will come on you, and the power of the Most High will overshadow you. So the holy one to be born will be called the Son of God.'"

The Holy Spirit fell on Jesus when He started His public ministry. Matthew 3:16 says: "As soon as Jesus was baptized, he went up out of the water. At that moment heaven was opened, and he saw the Spirit of God descending like a dove and alighting on him."

John 14-16 mention Jesus' last sermon, the Holy Spirit, to His disciple. John 14:16 says: "And I will ask the Father, and he will give you another advocate to help you and be with you forever."

John 14:26 says: "But the Advocate, the Holy Spirit, whom the Father will send in my name, will teach you all things and will remind you of everything I have said to you."

Jesus told His disciples that they must receive the Holy Spirit as He would enter their hearts and continue Jesus' work. We need to become men and women of the Holy Spirit throughout our lives.

Acts 1:4-5 says:

> On one occasion, while he was eating with them, he gave them this command: "Do not leave Jerusalem, but wait for the gift my Father promised, which you have heard me speak about. For John baptized with water, but in a few days you will be baptized with the Holy Spirit."

What we need the most is the fullness of the Holy Spirit. When we receive the Holy Spirit, the wonderful work of God will be done. Demons will be cast out. Diseases will be healed. Problems will be resolved. The miracles of God will be performed.

Before receiving the Holy Spirit, Peter disowned Jesus three times. After receiving the Holy Spirit, thousands of people heard Peter's sermon and put their faith in the Lord that day when he boldly preached the gospel.

When we're full of the Spirit, we become God's powerful servants. We live powerfully and victoriously in Christ. We become His witnesses.

Because we're filled with the Holy Spirit, we will also bear the fruit of the Spirit. Galatians 5:22-23 says that the fruit of the Holy Spirit is "love, joy, peace, forbearance, kindness, goodness, faithfulness, gentleness and self-control. Against such things there is no law."

3. We must be the ones with whom God is well pleased.

Matthew 3:17 says: "And a voice from heaven said, 'This is my Son, whom I love; with him I am well pleased.'"

Jesus Christ is the Son of God, whom God loves; with Him God is well pleased. At the same time, Jesus is God Himself. Even though Jesus is God Himself, He came to this earth in the flesh and opened the door of salvation for mankind. By doing so, He became the Savior.

Throughout His entire life on this earth for 33 years, Jesus gave delight to God. We should strive to be like Jesus and become servants whom God is pleased with.

There's a Korean firm "Aloe Maiim," whose mission statement is "please God and please people." Hae-Shil Hong, the CEO, worships God every week with all her employees in their company's meeting room from the beginning. Some criticize her but she faithfully holds onto her principles, striving to give delight to God through her company. Her company has grown quite splendidly. Now, it has 760 branches with more than 30,000 employees.

In Galatians 1:10, Apostle Paul said: "Am I now trying to win the approval of human beings, or of God? Or am I trying to please people? If I were still trying to please people, I would not be a servant of Christ." Instead of worrying about pleasing people, we need to focus on pleasing God only. He blesses us abundantly if we do so.

Strive to be God's servant that's humble, obedient, and full of the Holy Spirit. Give delight to the Lord and be greatly used by God.

Nomura Motoyuki, a Japanese pastor

Nomura Motoyuki, who is currently the pastor of Bethany Church in Yamanashi, Japan, is called "the saint for the poor" at Cheonggye Creek. He was awarded the honorary citizenship of Seoul for foreigners because he has made great contributions for the development of Seoul.

Nomura came to Korea in 1968 and was shocked by the horrible sight of poor people dying helplessly due to poverty and diseases. He immediately began to serve and preach the Gospel to the people in Korea. He first visited a crumbling shack in the slum area of Cheonggye Creek and he saw a girl lying in a small, pitch-dark room. Her knee bones and side bones were exposed and flies were sticking to her bones. Hatched maggots were eating her flesh. Nomura had to do something. He began to catch maggots but they penetrated into her flesh. She died two months later. Her death changed Nomura's life.

He traveled around the world and raised funds for the poor Koreans. For 20 years, he fed 2,000 poor Korean children. He sold his house in Tokyo and built a day care center in Cheonggye

Creek. He also imported seed cattle from New Zealand for the evicted residents who were forced to move to reclaimed land. He traveled to Korea 50 times until 1980s and transferred more than 75 million yens (equivalent to US $700,000) to Korea.

Nomura currently ministers in a home church in the mountain village in Yamanashi, Japan, living frugally and wearing second-hand clothes. He loves Korea so much that he wants to be buried in Korea. Nomura says:

> I came to understand little by little what Jesus wanted to say through the eyes of the dying girl. The poor people in Cheonggye Creek were the Bible teachers God sent me. There was the cross of Jesus, hope, and neighborly love. It was the best model of the kingdom of heaven for me. We didn't have to shout to see, hear, and know the love of Jesus Christ. I want to continue my work of service and sharing for the Koreans.

7

Following Jesus: Spirituality of Disciples

The spirituality of personal sanctification

19. With Christ

20. God Who Is Always with Us

21. The Chosen One

19

With Christ

I have been crucified with Christ and I no longer live, but Christ lives in me. The life I now live in the body, I live by faith in the Son of God, who loved me and gave himself for me. (Galatians 2:20)

The greatest grace and miracle that we can experience in our short lives is believing in Jesus. Salvation is the most blessed thing. We used to be enslaved to the devil, but after we've put our faith in Jesus, we've become God's beloved children. Because we're born again through faith in Jesus, we must live for the glory of God.

When Apostle Paul didn't know Jesus, he persecuted the church, but after meeting Him, his life was transformed. He confessed his faith in Galatians 2:20, saying: "I have been crucified with Christ and I no longer live, but Christ lives in me." He served the Lord throughout his life and held onto this confession. May Jesus, our Lord, be exalted in our lives! May we live victoriously in the Lord and enjoy true joy.

1. A faith in which I am dead

First, we need to approach God with self-denying faith. Galatians 2:20a says: "I have been crucified with Christ." We need to crucify our old self that belongs to sin and the flesh. We used to live in sin, but we were born again in Jesus.

Romans 6:6 says: "For we know that our old self was crucified with him so that the body ruled by sin might be done away with, that we should no longer be slaves to sin."

We know to not live as slaves to sin very well but it's difficult to practice. We're still too alive.

Paul was self-righteous and tried to practice his own justice. He persecuted the Christian church and was on the killers' side when Stephen was stoned to death. But after he laid down his life to Jesus, he began exalting Jesus alone and gave up his pride.

Philippians 3:8 says: "What is more, I consider everything a loss because of the surpassing worth of knowing Christ Jesus my Lord, for whose sake I have lost all things. I consider them garbage, that I may gain Christ."

Paul crucified everything he'd been proud of. When we aren't dead to sin, we get affected by other people's animosity. When we accept Jesus, our stubbornness, pride, disobedience, and hot temper are put to death.

We are the problem. Even though we think we've crucified ourselves, we come back to our sinful lives. Paul says the following about this problem in 1 Corinthians 15:31: "I face death every day—yes, just as surely as I boast about you in Christ Jesus our Lord."

Who is the "I" that should die every day? Our old selves, filled with hatred, fury, sin, unrighteousness, and debauchery, must die on the cross every day so that we can live as new creations. When we're driven by our old selves, we can't help but sin.

Romans 6:11 says: "In the same way, count yourselves dead to sin but alive to God in Christ Jesus." We must confess to the Lord: "I am dead to sin. My old self, which was filled with rage, hatred, and agony, is dead."

In Andrew Murray's book, *The Master's Indwelling*, he notes that one of the marks of a crucified man is helplessness:

> When a man says, "I am a crucified man, I am utterly helpless, every breath of life and strength must come from my Jesus," then we learn what it is to sink in our own impotence, and say, "I am nothing."[3]

Christian truth is called an ironic truth: when we die, we come back to life and when we try to live we die. Therefore, we must die every day. Because we're still so alive, we don't have peace in our lives.

We can't die by our own strength. We can only die when Jesus, whom we're united with, helps us crucify ourselves.

Romans 8:35 says: "Who shall separate us from the love of Christ? Shall trouble or hardship or persecution or famine or nakedness or danger or sword?" Since we're united with Jesus in His love, we can enter into God's wonderful grace in which we're dead with Jesus on the cross.

2. A faith in which Christ lives in us

Once we die with our Lord, we can have the faith in which Christ lives in us. Galatians 2:20b says: "I no longer live, but Christ lives in me." It's Jesus Christ who lives in us. The moment we believe in Jesus, our old self is put to death and we're renewed. 2 Corinthians 5:17 says: "Therefore, if anyone is in Christ, the new creation has come: The old has gone, the new is here!" We belong to God. We no longer live but Christ lives in us. Jesus is the Master of our lives.

We need to give glory to God in everything we do through our lives.

Romans 14:8 says: "If we live, we live for the Lord; and if we die, we die for the Lord. So, whether we live or die, we belong to the Lord." Whether we live or not, we do so for the Lord since He is within our hearts. The Lord of righteousness comes into our lives and makes us righteous. The holy Lord comes into our lives and makes us holy. The Lord of divine healing comes into our lives and heals us. The Lord of eternal life comes into our lives and leads us to eternal heaven.

The Lord Jesus is in your heart. He controls your life. So

commit your way to the Lord. When you commit everything to Him, He will work.

In John 3:30, John the Baptist said: "He must become greater; I must become less." Jesus must become greater in our lives and our old self must become less and less. As John confessed, we, too, must submit ourselves to the Lord and give glory to Jesus alone, being filled with the Word and the Holy Spirit.

3. The life of faith in Christ

After we've died and risen again with Christ, we must live by faith in Christ. Galatians 2:20b says: "The life I now live in the body, I live by faith in the Son of God, who loved me and gave himself for me."

I live by faith in the Son of God! I urge you to take steps with absolute faith in Jesus. Don't be too fixated on your surroundings or consequences, but fix your eyes on Jesus who is the pioneer and the perfecter of faith. Hebrews 11:6 tells us to march forward with faith: "And without faith it is impossible to please God, because anyone who comes to him must believe that he exists and that he rewards those who earnestly seek him."

We must live by faith in the Son of God, who loved us and gave himself for us. He loved us so much that He let His one and only Son Jesus die on the cross. Romans 8:32 says: "He who did not spare his own Son, but gave him up for us all—how will he not also, along with him, graciously give us all things?"

How precious the sacrifice and the love of Jesus is! He sacrificed Himself for each and every one of us. As God's children, we must live for His glory, amazed by His great sacrifice. No matter what kind of problems we may face, we're more than conquerors as long as we have faith in Jesus. Leave all your problems under the cross and look to Jesus. Then we can overcome all our problems.

Jesus' blood, which flowed from Calvary, will become a river of life. Jesus will be with us with His Spirit of Resurrection. Don't give up, rise up with faith. Focus on Jesus, who was crucified, and experience His marvelous miracles.

20

God Who Is Always with Us

Surely your goodness and love will follow me all the days of my life, and I will dwell in the house of the Lord forever. (Psalm 23:6)

There's a beginning and end in everything. We all die and many of us live in fear of that moment. But Christians aren't afraid of death because we gain the eternal life God gives the moment we believe in Jesus. When God calls us, we'll go to the new heaven and the new earth God has prepared for us.

John Milton, who wrote an epic poem *Paradise Lost*, once said: "Death is the golden key that opens the palace of eternity." To Christians, death isn't the end, but the new beginning of the world of eternal blessings. What kind of faith should we have in order to enjoy God's blessings, tasting eternal life, while living on this earth?

1. God is always with us.

Psalm 23:6a says: "Surely your goodness and love will follow me all the days of my life." Note the phrase "all the days of my life." Indeed, God is always with us throughout our lives. He takes care of us and pours His grace on us. That's because God is our shepherd and we're His sheep.

A shepherd always stays with his sheep. He takes care of them, protects them, satisfies their needs and loves them. He leads his sheep to green pastures so that they can graze grass as much as they can and leads them beside quiet waters so that they can drink water and rest there. He fights wild animals when they attack his sheep and protects them. He leads his sheep lest they should go astray or eat poisonous plants. He puts oil on them to keep them from harmful insect bites. When the sheep stay with their shepherd, they will find true satisfaction and joy.

David went through many hardships in his life, but he could overcome all his tribulations and gain victory because

God was always with him. In Psalm 23:4, David confessed: "For you are with me." David professed that the Lord God was with him at every moment of his life.

God was with the Israelites while they were going through the desert for 40 years after they had come out of Egypt. By day He went ahead of them in a pillar of cloud to guide them on their way and by night in a pillar of fire to give them light. He provided manna for them every day. He also sent quail when they wanted to eat meat. God provided for them sufficiently in their entire journey through the desert for 40 years.

In the same way, God will be with us as we go on this journey of life like He was with the Israelites in the wilderness. He'll pour out His enormous grace on us so that we won't lack anything but prosper spiritually, physically and environmentally. He renews our souls with the water of life that flows from the cross and fills us with the Holy Spirit every day so that we can live victoriously in this world. In the end, He will lead us to eternal heaven.

You're not alone. God is with you. Sometimes you may feel as if you're all alone when you face troubles, but God of love is with you.

2. God's goodness and love

Psalm 23:6a says: "Surely your goodness and love will follow me." God always provides His goodness and love for us. Here, the word "goodness" is the same as "God saw that it was good" in Genesis 1. God who always provides good things for us always walks with us and fills our lives with good things. This is the work of our good God.

"Love" in Psalm 23:6 means God's love for His chosen ones. His love is unconditional, never changing, and full of compassion. Not only does God provide good things for us daily but He also has compassion for us and overflows us with His love.

God's goodness and love always follows us all the days of our lives. When we walk towards the sun, our shadows follow us. Likewise, when we walk to God, His goodness and love follows us. We can't be separated from God.

Corrie ten Boom was a survivor from Nazi concentration camp during World War II. She traveled around the world and preached the gospel of forgiveness.

Corrie ten Boom and her family were sent to a concentration camp. Her father and sister died, but Corrie survived.

For many years, Corrie ten Boom traveled the world sharing her experience. More specifically, she shared her explanations for her experiences. She'd often speak with her head down. It looked like she was reading her notes, but she was actually working on a piece of needlepoint. Then, after telling her story of atrocities she experienced at the hands of the Nazis, Corrie would reveal the needlepoint she'd been working on. She'd hold up the backside, which was just a jumble of colors and threads with no discernible pattern. And she'd say: "That's how we see our lives. Sometimes it makes no sense." Then she'd turn the needlepoint over to reveal the finished side. And Corrie would conclude by saying: "This is how God views your life, and someday we will have the privilege of seeing it from His point of view."

We often see the wrong side, but God sees His side all the time. One day we'll see the embroidery from His side and thank Him.

Romans 8:28 says: "And we know that in all things God works for the good of those who love him, who have been called according to his purpose." All things—good or bad, joyful or sad—will work together to produce good results. And God will see that it is good. God takes care of us with His goodness and love. He works for our good in all things.

3. God prepares heaven for us.

Psalm 23:6b says: "I will dwell in the house of the Lord forever." David overcame all his hardships by looking to God, trusting that he'd dwell in the beautiful and eternal kingdom of heaven.

We'll enjoy true joy and peace in heaven, where there's no sorrow or teardrops. We'll dwell with God forever in heaven. So we need to look to heaven that God prepares for us. And when we do, we'll see that all the worry and fear will soon pass.

In 2 Corinthians 5:1, Paul said: "For we know that if the earthly tent we live in is destroyed, we have a building from God, an eternal house in heaven, not built by human hands." Paul was able to be faithful to Jesus through the end because he looked to heaven and didn't let persecutions affect him.

The Psalmist wrote about the meaninglessness of human life in Psalm 90:10: "Our days may come to seventy years, or eighty, if our strength endures; yet the best of them are but trouble and sorrow, for they quickly pass, and we fly away." Since our lives pass quickly, we don't have to worry about worldly things. Revelation 21:3-4 says:

> And I heard a loud voice from the throne saying, "Look! God's dwelling place is now among the people, and he will dwell with them. They will be his people, and God himself will be with them and be their God. He will wipe every tear from their eyes. There will be no more death or mourning or crying or pain, for the old order of things has passed away."

Let's look to heaven where there's no more pain, sorrow, crying, or mourning. Live faithfully in the Lord and concentrate on our eternal home: heaven. Let us give delight to God throughout our lives and share Jesus' love with as many people as we can.

Haven't you lived for no one but yourself your whole life? Live for God alone from now on and look to Him. He always wants to give you good things and He understands you. As you live a blessed life in Him, you can enjoy heaven today.

21

The Chosen One

> *Peter, an apostle of Jesus Christ, To God's elect, exiles scattered throughout the provinces of Pontus, Galatia, Cappadocia, Asia and Bithynia, who have been chosen according to the foreknowledge of God the Father, through the sanctifying work of the Spirit, to be obedient to Jesus Christ and sprinkled with his blood: Grace and peace be yours in abundance.* (1 Peter 1:1-2)

The First Epistle of Peter is called the epistle of hope. Peter wrote 1 Peter to comfort Christians that were under severe persecutions in the Roman Empire and to give them hope. They were living under severe persecutions in such a degree that being called "Christians" meant martyrdom. Despite everything, they dedicated themselves to the gospel without giving up their faith.

They kept their faith because they had the confidence that they were chosen by God. Even though they had to suffer for their faith, they were sure that they had the citizenship of heaven. Since they had this confidence, they could march forward with faith.

1. We are the pilgrims.

In 1 Peter 1:1, Peter called those who were scattered throughout the provinces of Pontus, Galatia, Cappadocia, Asia and Bithynia exiles (pilgrims in NKJV). We're exiles or pilgrims in this world because this world is not our permanent home.

Jesus also lived like a stranger in this world. Jesus, the King of kings and the Lord of lords, was born in a stall in Bethlehem and placed in a manger. We see beautiful pictures of the stall on Christmas cards but it wasn't beautiful—it was smelly and dirty. Moreover, Jesus never lived comfortably in a house. In Luke 9:58, Jesus said: "Foxes have dens and birds have nests, but the Son of Man has no place to lay his head."

He was stripped and beaten so badly that blood covered His face. He died a horrible death on the cross. Even after death, He was laid in somebody else's tomb temporarily and was resurrected on the third day. He lived a life of a total pilgrim.

Jacob was presented before Pharaoh of Egypt after meeting his son Joseph. He said to Pharaoh: "The years of my pilgrimage are a hundred and thirty. My years have been few and difficult, and they do not equal the years of the pilgrimage of my fathers" (Genesis 47:9). Moses said in Psalm 90:10: "Our days may come to seventy years, or eighty, if our strength endures; yet the best of them are but trouble and sorrow, for they quickly pass, and we fly away." The forefathers of faith also lived like wanderers and their pilgrimage lives quickly passed by.

Who can give us true satisfaction, joy, or happiness when we're strangers to this world? Who can understand and comfort our pain we experience as pilgrims? There is only one person: Jesus Christ, our Savior, who lived as a stranger Himself in this world. He always walks with us and He alone knows all our sorrows. Jesus alone is the true comforter and healer. So trust in Jesus, our good friend, and look forward to heaven, our eternal home.

2. The work of God

1 Peter 1:2a says: "Who have been chosen according to the foreknowledge of God the Father, through the sanctifying work of the Spirit." God controls our life. What's even more amazing is that God knew us before He created the world.

Ephesians 1:4-5 says: "For he chose us in him before the creation of the world to be holy and blameless in his sight. In love he predestined us for adoption to sonship through Jesus Christ, in accordance with his pleasure and will." God has chosen us before the creation of the world and adopted us as His children through Jesus.

Jesus said in John 15:16: "You did not choose me, but I chose you and appointed you." It's not by our own strength or choice that we follow Jesus and become God's children; God chose and called us first. So even when we feel broken during our journey as pilgrims, we can overcome our problems through our faith in the One who chose us.

God sends the Holy Spirit to us to make us holy, which means set apart. Holiness means separation from the world, sin, and our old self. The Spirit enters us so that we may steer clear from evil and bear fruits.

1 Thessalonians 4:3a says: "It is God's will that you should be sanctified." 1 Peter 1:15 also says: "But just as he who called you is holy, so be holy in all you do." It is God's will that we are holy, and therefore, as the chosen people of God, we must live a holy life.

Gary Thomas, an American evangelist and president of the Center for Evangelical Spirituality, said in his book, *The Beautiful Fight*, that holiness is "allowing [the] Holy Spirit to manifest himself through us, transforming us to see, hear, think, and feel as the ascended Christs [does]."[4]

The ultimate purpose of holiness is to become like Jesus. In other words, it is for us to be the salt and the light in this world as little Jesus.

3. Advance of Faith

1 Peter 1:2b says: "To be obedient to Jesus Christ and sprinkled with his blood." As the chosen people of God, we must obey Jesus and march forward with steadfast faith.

Hebrew 5:8-9 says: "Son though he was, he learned obedience from what he suffered and, once made perfect, he became the source of eternal salvation for all who obey him." Jesus completed the work of salvation for us by obeying God the Father and becoming the source of eternal salvation for all who obey Him. When we obey Jesus, He will heal every aspect of our lives.

As God's chosen people, we need to trust in the power of Jesus' blood every day because it helps us overcome the world and leads us to a life full of the Spirit. Not only that, we're able to fight and defeat the devil through the power of His blood. Revelation 12:11 says: "They triumphed over him by the blood of the Lamb and by the word of their testimony; they did not love their lives so much as to shrink from death." His blood and power alone will lead us to victory in our spiritual warfare.

Lewis Hartsough, a Methodist evangelist, devoted himself in his ministry but he was spiritually thirsty. He experienced Jesus' grace and power of His blood when he was leading a revival.

He wrote down his enthusiasm and deep impression:

I hear Thy welcome voice,

> That calls me, Lord, to Thee,
> For cleansing in Thy precious blood
> That flowed on Calvary.
>
> ...
>
> Though coming weak and vile,
> Thou dost my strength assure;
> Thou dost my vileness fully cleanse,
> Till spotless all, and pure.[5]

Experience the power of Jesus' blood. Your spirits will be renewed and you'll have wonderful changes in your life.

What's our hope as pilgrims in this world? It is to look to Jesus and heaven. Don't be discouraged just because you've encountered some problem, but trust in God. Thank Him for choosing you. Thank Him for His grace and love.

Trust in the power of Jesus' blood that sets us free from sin and leads us to be filled with the Holy Spirit. God will work miraculous wonders when you walk with Him every day and obey Him.

Amazing Grace

One of the songs that are most popular among Christians and non-Christians alike is "Amazing Grace," written by John Newton.

Newton was nurtured by a Christian mother who taught him the Bible at an early age, but he was raised in his father's image after she died of tuberculosis when John was 7. At age 11, Newton went on his first sea-voyage. He became a violent man since then. He became the captain of a slave trade ship, capturing Africans and selling them as slaves in the slave markets of England and Europe. He was so cruel that he shot rebellious slaves, killed them, and threw them into the sea.

In 1748, he was on the slave trade ship on his way back to England. The ship encountered a severe storm. The storm was so severe that the ship almost wrecked. Being afraid of imminent death, he knelt down and prayed to God, saying, "God, I am worthless and do not deserve your mercy. But I plead with you. Have mercy on me, then I will become a new person, I promise."

Newton prayed with tears, remembering the prayers of his mother at his early age. Then the storm died down and, on the eighteenth day, he was rescued and returned to England safely.

This experience of conversion began to change Newton. He heard the sermon of John Whitfield, the famous evangelist and powerful preacher in those days, and wanted to serve the Lord for the rest of his life as a priest.

In 1764, at the age of 39, Newton was ordained as a priest and began his ministry. He often began his sermon, "Drunkards or libertines are not so bad compared to me." His testimony touched many people's hearts.

Upon hearing the sermons of John Wesley who was against

the slave trade, he became an abolitionist, preaching against the slave trade. He went to people and tried to persuade them that the slave trade was against God's will. William Wilberforce, a British politician, was affected by Newton. Wilberforce introduced and brought a bill calling for abolition more than 150 times to the Parliament of England until the passage of the Slave Trade Act of 1807. Newton lived to see this before his death in 1807.

John Newton wrote more than 300 hymns and "Amazing Grace" is like his autobiographical hymn. He wrote the following prayer at the age of 54.

> Amazing Grace! How sweet the sound,
> That saved a wretch like me!
> I once was lost, but now am found
> Was blind, but now I see

He made the following confession in his last sermon when he was 82.

"My beloved brothers and sisters, my memory is becoming dim. But I clearly remember two things. One is that I was the worst sinner in the past. The other is that God did not forsake me nonetheless but had mercy on me. He saved me through Jesus Christ."

8

Following Jesus: Spirituality of Disciples

The spirituality of missionary work

22. The Hope of Resurrection

23. Mission

24. March forward with Dreams and Hope

22

The Hope of Resurrection

But Christ has indeed been raised from the dead, the firstfruits of those who have fallen asleep. For since death came through a man, the resurrection of the dead comes also through a man. For as in Adam all die, so in Christ all will be made alive. But each in turn: Christ, the firstfruits; then, when he comes, those who belong to him. Then the end will come, when he hands over the kingdom to God the Father after he has destroyed all dominion, authority and power. For he must reign until he has put all his enemies under his feet. The last enemy to be destroyed is death. (1 Corinthians 15:20-26)

Jesus was raised from the dead and destroyed the power of death. His resurrection is the greatest miracle, blessing, and grace in human history. He conquered death and destroyed the power of sin and death. This signifies that Jesus is the Master of life and death.

1 Corinthians 15:14 says: "And if Christ has not been raised, our preaching is useless and so is your faith." If Jesus hadn't resurrected, our faith would be meaningless. It wouldn't be able to exercise any power or change anyone and our hope wouldn't be fulfilled.

But luckily, Jesus did rise up from death and He is still alive and working. Since the resurrected Lord Jesus is with us, the resurrection power continues to work today in the same way as it did back then.

1. Resurrected Jesus is the firstfruits of those who have fallen asleep.

1 Corinthians 15:20 says: "But Christ has indeed been raised from the dead, the firstfruits of those who have fallen asleep."

No one in the world is free from the problem of sin and death. Romans 3:23 says: "For all have sinned and fall short of the glory of God." Romans 6:23a also says: "For the wages of sin is death."

We're hopeless beings. We were born in sin, living in sin and dying in sin. No one in this world can solve this problem.

Jesus Christ is the only person who can solve this problem. Even though He's God Himself, He came to this earth in the flesh and died on the cross, taking all our sins, diseases, curses, and even death. When Jesus said, "it is finished," all our sins in the past, present and future are forgiven by the virtue of His blood. Now, whoever believes in Jesus will turn into a righteous being since His blood covers all the sins of those who believe in Him. Therefore, we can triumphantly and confidently approach God's throne.

Jesus was resurrected on the third day and stayed on earth for 40 days, appearing to His disciples and others. 1 Corinthians 15:20 says that Jesus Christ has become the firstfruits of those who've fallen asleep. To fall asleep implies to wake up again. Our lives don't end when we die; we'll live again with the life of resurrection.

Yes, we'll die when the time comes, but it's not the end. Nonbelievers struggle with the concept of death because they think it's the end. But to believers, death is a new beginning.

We rise up again from death, following Jesus, the firstfruits of those who have fallen asleep.

"First" is a very important prefix here. God commanded the Israelites to give Him the firstfruits of the crops they sowed in the field. It signifies that people must acknowledge the sovereignty of God. By giving the firstfruits to God, we confess that everything has come from God. So by God's grace, all who believe in Jesus will participate in the resurrection.

Romans 8:11 says: "And if the Spirit of him who raised Jesus from the dead is living in you, he who raised Christ from the dead will also give life to your mortal bodies because of his Spirit who lives in you."

Therefore, we must march forward with faith, holding onto the Lord Jesus alone.

2. Death and resurrection

1 Corinthians 15:21-22 says: "For since death came through a man, the resurrection of the dead comes also through a man. For as in Adam all die, so in Christ all will be made alive."

When Adam, the forefather of mankind, sinned, mankind was condemned. But through Jesus' death and resurrection, we can participate in His glory through our faith.

Romans 5:18 says: "Consequently, just as one trespass resulted in condemnation for all people, so also one righteous act resulted in justification and life for all people." Since Jesus took all our sins and died on the cross, all who believe in Jesus will gain life.

The life of Jesus' resurrection is eternal. Our life in the flesh comes to an end when the time comes, but the life of resurrection is eternal. In John 11:25, Jesus said: "I am the resurrection and the life. The one who believes in me will live, even though they die." We've become great victors in Jesus, and death, diseases, poverty, or curses have no power over us.

When Jesus comes again, all believers on earth will be caught up in the clouds to meet Jesus in the air. 1 Thessalonians 4:16 says: "For the Lord himself will come down from heaven, with a loud command, with the voice of the archangel and with the trumpet call of God, and the dead in Christ will rise first." At the final judgment, death will be destroyed forever. 1 Corinthians 15:26 says: "The last enemy to be destroyed is death."

We don't have to fear death because we've already received

the spirit of resurrection and the blessing of eternal life. We must be used greatly by God with the hope of eternal heaven.

3. The mission that God entrusts to us

1 Corinthians 15:58 says: "Therefore, my dear brothers and sisters, stand firm. Let nothing move you. Always give yourselves fully to the work of the Lord, because you know that your labor in the Lord is not in vain."

This is the conclusion of 1 Corinthians 15, which is called the chapter of resurrection. This chapter tells us how we—who have the life of resurrection—should live on this earth. We must give ourselves fully to Lord's work that is pleasing to Him.

The work that our Lord delights in is being Jesus' witness and preaching the gospel. We should go to the impoverished, poorly clothed, hungry, hurt and wounded. We must proclaim that all their problems will be resolved and that God's healing and forgiveness will come into their lives when the resurrected Lord is with them.

So-Hyun Baik is the office manager of the Nation Love Community. She's been ministering to the homeless in front of Yongsan Station for 14 years. When she was praying to God when her husband failed in his business, God told her to serve her neighbors who were in deep distress.

So she cooked pumpkin soup for the homeless near Yongsan Station and preached the gospel to them. Many people began to change. When they got jobs in various fields, they gave their tithe and founded the Nation Love Community. They serve the homeless and provide food for 400 people a day near Seoul Station.

Baik said, "Since I myself went through sufferings, I know what it is to serve our neighbors and to give thanks. I can see resurrection beyond suffering by looking at the homeless who received hope in hopelessness."

1 Corinthians 10:31 says: "So whether you eat or drink or whatever you do, do it all for the glory of God." Have you lived only for yourself so far? If so, start living for the glory of God.

23

Mission

When they had finished eating, Jesus said to Simon Peter, "Simon son of John, do you love me more than these?" "Yes, Lord," he said, "you know that I love you." Jesus said, "Feed my lambs." Again Jesus said, "Simon son of John, do you love me?" He answered, "Yes, Lord, you know that I love you." Jesus said, "Take care of my sheep." The third time he said to him, "Simon son of John, do you love me?" Peter was hurt because Jesus asked him the third time, "Do you love me?" He said, "Lord, you know all things; you know that I love you." Jesus said, "Feed my sheep." (John 21:15-17)

People want to be happy and successful, but we can't bring happiness to our own lives no matter how hard we try. True happiness can be attained only in Jesus.

Peter left Jesus and tried to live on his own but his life was a total failure. But Jesus came to him and gave him a new mission that changed his life completely. He used to be a weak disciple, denying Jesus, but he turned into God's great servant and lived for Jesus alone.

We can live happily and meaningfully only when we follow His work with dreams and hope.

1. Peter betrayed Jesus.

Peter was the leader of Jesus' disciples; he followed Him closely and worked hard. He even claimed with confidence that he would never desert Jesus and that he would never disown Jesus even if he had to die with Him. Matthew 26:33 says: "Peter replied, 'Even if all fall away on account of you, I never will.'"

But when Jesus was arrested, Peter disowned Him three times. On the third time, he even swore that he didn't know Jesus. Matthew 26:74 says: "Then he began to call down curses, and he swore to them, 'I don't know the man!' Immediately a rooster crowed."

After that, Peter remembered the word Jesus had spoken: "Before the rooster crows, you will disown me three times," and wept bitterly (Matthew 26:34).

We too sometimes deny or betray Jesus while saying that we believe in Him. We get carried away with material wealth, power and fame while we claim that we love Jesus the most. We lie for our own benefit and we hate. When we say we love but do all these things, we're disowning Jesus.

Jesus watches us with eyes like blazing fire. We need to go back to the moment when we first met Jesus—when we were pure and childlike. We should love Him without ever-changing and live a life that's pleasing to the Lord.

2. Jesus was looking for Peter.

Peter felt remorse even after he met Jesus. He was so frustrated that he forgot his mission and went back to the life as a fisherman. John 21:3 says: "'I'm going out to fish,' Simon Peter told them, and they said, 'We'll go with you.' So they went out and got into the boat, but that night they caught nothing."

Peter threw his nets over and over again but caught nothing. Three years ago, when he experienced a similar situation, he said to Jesus: "Master, we've worked hard all night and haven't caught anything. But because you say so, I will let down the nets" (Luke 5:5).

When we turn away from the Lord, we won't catch anything no matter how hard we work. We'll end up with empty nets and boats. If Jesus is absent from our lives, we won't gain anything but emptiness.

The day began to break at the Sea of Tiberias and it was time for them to go back. Peter was probably devastated and it was then that Jesus called him. John 21:4 says: "Early in the morning, Jesus stood on the shore, but the disciples did not realize that it was Jesus."

Jesus comes to us when we fail or when we're frustrated. He comforts us and wipes our tears when we cry in deep pain and agony. Jesus raises us up, healing and renewing us.

Jesus said to Peter and other disciples who were in deep despair: "Throw your net on the right side of the boat and you will find some" (John 21:6). When they did, they weren't able to haul the net in because so many fish were there. When we obey

Jesus as Peter did, miracles will happen; our empty boats will be full of fish and our problems will be solved.

3. Jesus gives a mission

As soon as he heard that it was Jesus, Peter wrapped his outer garment around him and jumped into the water, swimming to the shore. He arrived at the shore and saw a fire of burning coals there with fish on it and some bread.

Jesus didn't excoriate Peter even though he'd disowned Him. Instead, He prepared fire to warm Peter who was shivering and dripping water. He also prepared some food for He knew that Peter would be hungry after working through the night, and Peter ate while weeping. The fire reminded him of the night of his betrayal—he had disowned Him three times in front of a fire. But Jesus prepared a fire for Peter and forgave him in front of it. This shows the unchanging love of Jesus. He comforted Peter with His love.

After they'd finished eating, Jesus asked Peter a question. John 21:15 says: "When they had finished eating, Jesus said to

Simon Peter, 'Simon son of John, do you love me more than these?' 'Yes, Lord,' he said, 'you know that I love you.' Jesus said, 'Feed my lambs.'"

Jesus asked Peter if he loved Him three times because He wanted to heal the hurts in his heart. Disowning Jesus three times left an indelible scar in Peter's mind. So Jesus gave Peter a chance to confess "I love you Lord," three times.

After that, Jesus gave Peter a mission. The first mission Jesus gave to Peter was to feed His lambs. Here, lambs represent new converts in the church whose faith is still weak. Jesus wants us to feed the new converts with the Word of God so that their faith will grow and so that they will stand firm on their faith.

The second mission Jesus gave to Peter was to take care of His sheep. Here, the sheep represent Christians. Jesus told Peter to protect and serve them. Jesus wants to protect Christians so that they won't conform to false teachings, heresies, or the temptations of the world. He also wants us to serve and take care of those who are in despair or need.

Jesus' love never changes. Even if we've gone into the world, as long as we come back to Him, He takes us back and holds us with His love. He reinstates us and gives us a new mission like He gave Peter a new mission: that we should take care of our neighbors who are poor, neglected, poorly clothed, or hungry. We need to give our lives to Jesus and follow this mission. We need to go and tell people about Jesus' love.

24

March forward with Dreams and Hope

Now there were four men with leprosy at the entrance of the city gate. They said to each other, "Why stay here until we die? If we say, 'We'll go into the city'—the famine is there, and we will die. And if we stay here, we will die. So let's go over to the camp of the Arameans and surrender. If they spare us, we live; if they kill us, then we die." At dusk they got up and went to the camp of the Arameans. When they reached the edge of the camp, no one was there, for the Lord had caused the Arameans to hear the sound of chariots and horses and a great army, so that they said to one another, "Look, the king of Israel has hired the Hittite and Egyptian kings to attack us!" So they got up and fled in the dusk and abandoned their tents and their horses and donkeys. They left the camp as it was and ran for their lives. The men who had leprosy reached the edge of the camp, entered one of the tents and ate and drank. Then

they took silver, gold and clothes, and went off and hid them. They returned and entered another tent and took some things from it and hid them also. Then they said to each other, "What we're doing is not right. This is a day of good news and we are keeping it to ourselves. If we wait until daylight, punishment will overtake us. Let's go at once and report this to the royal palace." So they went and called out to the city gatekeepers and told them, "We went into the Aramean camp and no one was there—not a sound of anyone—only tethered horses and donkeys, and the tents left just as they were."
(2 Kings 7:3-10)

We often encounter difficulties. As Christians, even when we're on the edge of a precipice, we should never give up. Since Jesus, our Lord, is our eternal hope, life, and joy, we must lift up our eyes and hold onto the cross. We need to behold the Lord.

The four men with leprosy were in deep distress but they marched forward with faith and experienced a great miracle. They also spread this good news to many people.

1. Those who were in despair

In the days of Prophet Elisha, Ben-Hadad, the king of Aram, mobilized his entire army and marched up and laid siege to Samaria. Instead of fighting, he chose to seize the city for a long time, cutting all supplies into the city. Consequently, there was a great famine in the city and people were dying of hunger. The famine was beyond description and so severe that some people even ate their own children.

There were four men with leprosy near the city. In those days, when a man had leprosy, he was isolated. Anyone with a defiling disease had to live alone and outside the village. So they built a shack outside the city wall and begged people that passed the city gate for food. Now the city gate was closed and no one went in or came out of the city.

Instead of giving up or slumping down in times of dire trouble, they chose to follow their dreams and hope. 2 Kings 7:3-4 says:

> Now there were four men with leprosy at the entrance of the city gate. They said to each other, "Why stay here until

we die? If we say, 'We'll go into the city'—the famine is there, and we will die. And if we stay here, we will die. So let's go over to the camp of the Arameans and surrender. If they spare us, we live; if they kill us, then we die."

They knew that they'd die when they went into the city due to starvation, and they'd also die if they stayed there. The only thing they could do was to go over to the camp of the Arameans to surrender and hope that they'd spare their lives.

In the same way, when you encounter problems, look to Jesus and have hope. Have faith that the Lord of love is with you, that He will help you and that He alone can solve all your difficulties.

2. We must take the steps of faith with dreams and hope

Now, the four men with leprosy marched with dreams and hope. 2 Kings 7:5 says: "At dusk they got up and went to the camp of the Arameans. When they reached the edge of the camp, no one was there."

Leprosy is a long-term infection by the bacteria Mycobacterium leprae, which results in tissue loss, and causes their body parts to degenerate and fall off. This damage may result in a lack of ability to feel pain, which can lead to more loss of the body parts from injuries or infection. Spiritually speaking, these men with leprosy refer to mankind who is dying due to sin. However, when we have hope by believing in Jesus, we can see the way to the solution.

It is God's will to give dreams and hope to us. Jeremiah 29:11 says: "'For I know the plans I have for you,' declares the Lord, 'plans to prosper you and not to harm you, plans to give you hope and a future.'"

To Christians, there's no more hopelessness or the fear of death because Jesus, our eternal hope, is with us. We can live as more than conquerors in the Lord and gain victory every day. Change your perspective so that you can live with absolute, positive faith and thanksgiving. Don't give up. Stand up with faith instead and fight through your problems.

3. God's help

When the four men went over to the camp of the Arameans, God's hand was with them. Something miraculous happened: the Lord made the Arameans hear sounds of chariots and horses rather than the lepers. So the Arameans got up and ran for their lives. 2 Kings 7:6-7 says:

> For the Lord had caused the Arameans to hear the sound of chariots and horses and a great army, so that they said to one another, "Look, the king of Israel has hired the Hittite and Egyptian kings to attack us!" So they got up and fled in the dusk and abandoned their tents and their horses and donkeys. They left the camp as it was and ran for their lives.

Those men with leprosy must have stumbled and since they were infected and hungry, they couldn't have marched like a great army. But the Arameans heard what God made them hear so they fled the camp. When the four men reached the edge of the camp, there wasn't anyone there. They found a lot of food there so they ate and drank.

We may look weak to people but we're strong because God is with us. When we take a step of faith, all hopelessness will flee from us and God's blessings will come to us. So don't give up because the Lord Almighty is with you.

4. Good news that we must preach

When they ate and drank fully enough, the men with leprosy came to their senses. What they were doing was wrong: people were dying of hunger in the city. 2 Kings 7:9 says:

> Then they said to each other, "What we're doing is not right. This is a day of good news and we are keeping it to ourselves. If we wait until daylight, punishment will overtake us. Let's go at once and report this to the royal palace."

So they went, called out to the city gatekeepers and told them about this good news. Then the people went out and plundered the camp of the Arameans. They also experienced

God's grace and were able to eat and drink.

We must spread the good and beautiful news all around. The best and happiest news is that Jesus died on the cross to save sinners. Nothing is a greater news than this. When we preach this good news, the hopeless and oppressed will find hope. Those who are on the verge of death will find the hope for eternal life and resurrection. Those who are swamped with problems will find enough strength and courage to come out of the swamp.

God wants to fill our lives with His grace and blessings. There will be miracles when we hold onto God's promises and march forward with faith. We'll experience even more when we spread the good news. Let's enjoy a blessed life, filled with dreams and hopes in the Lord.

Bruce Olson

Brue Olson ventured into Venezuela's uncharted jungles to preach the gospel to the native tribes in South America.

When he was 14, Olson put himself before Jesus while reading the New Testament, and when he was 16, he felt that God wanted him to become a missionary to the Indians of South America.

He enrolled in Pennsylvania State university and transferred to the University of Minnesota a year later to study linguistics. When he was 19, despite his parents' objection, Olson left college and went to Venezuela without missionary training, organization or support. He trusted in God alone; he'd heard about the Motilones and their violent clashes with oil company employees seeking to drill their land. He felt convicted to help the most dangerous tribe in the South American jungles, who threw orphans to leopards and didn't care for the elders.

Olson was seized by the Motilones. He was whipped and pierced by arrow tips. He suffered from hunger and diseases. But after going through these sufferings, he was able to live with them. Through Olson, the Motilones received the gospel and began to change into the image of Jesus.

The same Motilones that killed people mercilessly started to adopt orphans and cared for their elders when they met Jesus. They built their first health centers, schools, and cooperative unions. Through these facilities, they made contributions to the development of Colombia as well as their own tribe.

Olson's missionary work that was full of toil caused the most vicious tribe changed into the core preacher in their society.

Once, he was kidnapped by the rebels. He was struck by a pistol shot in his chest, leg and neck. He was tied to a tree in a jungle for four months. During this time, he taught the guerillas how to cook and how to read and write. He also gave them dental treatment. As a result, 120 guerillas accepted Jesus.

Olson has lived as the friend of the Motilones for more than 50 years. Even though he's constantly under threat, he still lives with the Motilones in the jungles.

Olson says that this is possible because God is with Him.

He says: "it was God who brought me here. I couldn't have come by myself. I couldn't have fought all problems, loneliness or dangers. If I hadn't experienced the strong and decisive presence of God, I couldn't have left home."

References

1. Kyle Idleman, Not a Fan (Grand Rapids, Zondervan, 2016), 25.
2. Thomas Á Kempis, The Imitation of Christ (Boston, Pauline Books & Media, 2015), 123.
3. Andrew Murray, Thee Master's Indwelling (Radford, Wilder, 2018), 63
4. Gary Thomas, The Beautiful Fight (Grand Rapids, Zondervan, 2007), 166.
5. Lewis Hartsough, "I Hear Thy Welcome Voice," 1872, hymn.

Medicine. [in Korean] The Dream, 2013.
- Koh, Hoon, et al. The Elders who Move the Hearts of the Pastors. [in Korean] Korean Literature Mission Society, 2007.
- Lee, Young Hoon. The Holy Spirit Movement: the History of the Assemblies of God. [in Korean] Seoul Logos, 2014.
- Maxwell, John C. The Preacher's Commentary—OT Old Testament. Vol. 5. Nashville: Thomas Nelson, 2004.
- Nomura, Motoyuki. Nomura Report. [in Korean] Noonbit, 2013.
- Oh, So-Woon. Researches on Hymns in the 21st Century. [in Korean] The Bible House, 2011.
- Olson, Bruce. Bruchko. Charisma House, 2006.
- Park, Yong-Kyu. The Pyongyang Great Revival. [in Korean] Word of Life Press, 2000.
- _____ Korean Church History. [in Korean] The Institute of Korean Christian History, 2004.
- Shin, Yong-Won. "The Fruit of Adversities." [in Korean] Kookmin Daily News, 2015.
- Thomas, Gary. The Beautiful Fight Surrendering to the Transforming Presence of God Every Day of Your Life. Zondervan, 2007.
- Yang, Young-Jo. Education of Korean Contemporary History, Vol 3: the Korean War. [in Korean] National Museum of Korean Contemporary History, 2014.

BIBLIOGRAPHY

- A Kempis, Thomas. The Imitation of Christ. Milwaukee: Bruce Publishing Company, 1949.
- Baik, So-Hyun. "I Understand Thanksgiving after Suffering." [in Korean] Kookmin Daily News, 2013.
- Batterson, Mark. Soulprint: Discovering Your Divine Destiny. Multnomah, 2011.
- Galli, Mark. Francis of Assisi and His World. Westmont: IVP, 2002.
- Hong, Hae-Shil. "In the Light and Salt." [in Korean] Kookmin Daily News, 2004.
- Idleman, Kyle. Not a Fan. Zondervan Publishing House, 2016.
- Jones, Stanley E, Eunice Jones Matthews. The Divine Yes. Abingdon Press, 1992.
- Kim, Kwang-Soo. Korean Christian History. [in Korean] Christian Literature Press, 1974.
- Kim, Woo-Sung. Chimney Prayer. [in Korean] Peniel, 2019.
- Kim, Yang-Kyu. Another Level of Healing, Biblical Oriental